LILLIAN TOO

LIVING WITH
GOOD FENG SHUI

KONSEPBOOKS
ASTROLOGY . FENG SHUI . INSPIRATIONS

Contents

Welcome to my home,
A place of comfort for me and my family...
Here is where my Energy is balanced
And harmony and peace prevail,
Where growth is steady, silent and sure,
And prosperity creeps in through many doorways.

Where our love for each other
And for the larger world increasingly expands,
Where our minds, our bodies and our spirits soar to
Great heights of joyousness...
We feel contentment daily.

My home has become a Pure Land
Shared with dogs, fish, squirrels,
Birds, plants, trees, flowers and many friends.
There is laughter... Continuous,
Sunshine... Fantastic,
There are sounds, mantras, music,
Bells and drums and the patter of tiny feet,
There are many nice things, activating, energizing.

Grandsons visit daily, bring pure yang chi,
My Goldens and Cockers love me unconditionally,
Doorbell Rings, Visitors come,
Home Abuzz, Alive, Good Vibes flowing,
Breezes blow, Sunlight filters
Starry night skies bring the new and full moon,
Yin mingles freely with Yang,
Rain brings big drops of water.

And continuous feel-good, good fortune...
Welcome to my home,
Which has been part of my life for over 30 years.
Let me embrace you with my energy,
Share with you some high and low moments of my life,
As well as many beneficial discoveries...

Opening Notes

Above: **With Jennifer, celebrating the Complete Illustrated Guide To Feng Shui becoming the number 1 bestseller in Barnes & Noble Bookstores in the USA in the summer of 1997.**

Above: **The annual Fortune & Feng Shui series I write with Jennifer. Here, displayed in Barnes & Noble bookstore in Hawaii, America.**

Facing Page: **My early thoughts on my new career... extracted from an old album. But as we go to print this November 2009, I have just been conferred the title of GRAND MASTER by the International Feng Shui Society of Singapore.**

Back then in 1997, the Western media described the revival of interest in feng shui that followed the success of my first overseas-published book, *The Complete Illustrated Guide To Feng Shui* (CIG) which became the summer bestseller in Barnes and Noble bookstores in America in 1997, as "massive in the United States, huge Down Under, big in the UK… and as common as chopsticks in Hong Kong."

The international success of my full-colour illustrated book published as a hardback by a UK publisher, Element Books Ltd eventually led to an explosion of worldwide interest on the subject that kept getting bigger and bigger. That book became a worldwide phenomenon and was translated into 31 languages. My publisher was ecstatic with the success of the book and quickly commissioned more books from me. But so did many other publishers. Feng shui became very trendy and in no time at all, where before there were hardly any books on the subject, suddenly bookstores around the world had entire aisles devoted to feng shui books.

What had started out as a hobby writing about a passion of mine suddenly opened a new profession for me as a writer. I went with the flow and eventually the subject took on a life on its own and I was swept along by the momentum. Worldwide demand for my books kept increasing and I signed on with more publishers. I wrote several worldwide bestsellers for the Random House Imprint **Rider Books** and also wrote for **Harper Collins** and a couple of other publishers. It was the stuff of dreams and I barely had time to catch my breath. But the more I wrote, the more fulfilled and happy I became. Internationally, the subject drew a generally favourable press.

In a big story devoted to the rise and rise of feng shui at that time, UK's Cosmopolitan magazine reported that many celebrities had jumped on the feng shui bandwagon - people like **Richard Branson**, the flamboyant Virgin Airlines boss; **Boy George** the pop singer whose love life was disastrous until he got the feng shui man in; the all-time star and writer **Shirley MacLaine** who had to bring the feng shui man to rearrange her furniture as her life had got too cluttered. And after the makeover, of course, the erstwhile Ms MacLaine enjoyed a resurgence in her career.

There are others of course; corporations that ranged from the serious mandarins of the **Hong Kong Bank** to the managers of **Marks and Spencer.** I myself knew of many more famous names that used feng shui to insure against bad luck, especially in Hong Kong and Taiwan, where belief in feng shui is quite commonplace.

In the West, growing interest in feng shui stemmed in part from the opening of China. Hong Kong was reverting back to China rule in 1997, and during that time, many things Chinese had become very trendy, not just feng shui but also Traditional Chinese Medicine, Tai Chi, Kung Fu martial arts, Sun Tzu's Art of War and Chinese Destiny Analysis comprising Palmistry and Face Reading… but the popularity of feng shui surpassed them all. Feng shui seemed to touch a chord in

Me ? . . . a fengshui expert ?

the collective unconscious of the world then, and I was just lucky to find myself right at the heart of this revival of interest in an ancient living skill.

But what a wonderful surprise - it seemed that overnight I had a new profession! I had always wanted to become a bestselling writer, so this sudden development in my life at a time when I had "retired" from corporate working life and wanting to take things easy, became something I embraced passionately and with great enthusiasm.

For several years after that, I travelled to the capital cities of the world - to London, New York, San Francisco, Sydney, Tokyo - all over to popularize feng shui and to promote my books. Soon I was getting invited by international organizations, clubs, corporations to speak and to consult… because that wonderful book, my first international effort, went on to sell millions of copies, thereby spearheading a major revival of interest in feng shui.

At that time I was living a life of blissful retirement, enjoying my role as a fulltime mother to Jennifer. I had cashed out investments in Hong Kong, sold my properties and businesses there to return to my family in Malaysia. Jennifer was 11 when I came back and when all this feng shui thingy was happening, I was commuting between London and Malaysia because Jennifer was at boarding school in the UK and I wanted to attend her school functions. So it actually worked out very well for me.

My success as a writer should not have surprised me. It had been brought to me by the excellent feng shui of my house then - the same house I had left in 1982 to relocate to Hong Kong, and which I returned to in 1991 after cashing out everything in Hong Kong! My home felt very sad when I returned. It had obviously missed me all those years I had been away… I remember telling Jennifer, "The house looks really shabby darling," and I had shaken my head sadly.

Then Jennifer said, "But Mummy, now you are back, you can make it nice again!" And she stared up at me with very bright, trusting eyes, my 11 year old. Actually, my returning to Malaysia had also been prompted by her. On one of her regular trips to Hong Kong to visit with me, she had said at the airport, "Mummy why are we always saying goodbye?"

That statement did horrible things to my head; and I believe it sort of consciously or unconsciously caused me to set in motion events that would eventually lead me to look for a buyer for my department store business, persuade my partners to cash out, and finally to return home to Malaysia. It was a tough decision but it sort of got made. And although selling one's business at a profit is not always easy to make happen, somehow I managed to do it - aided no doubt by my five arowana fish and the good feng shui of my Hong Kong apartment!

So I successfully sold everything and returned home to Malaysia. To do so, I had to unwind my business and property investments, uproot a very glamourous life style and basically turn my back on the excitement of corporate-style high living. That was a big decision, but in later years looking back, in spite of the occasional pang of regret at giving it all up, truly that was the best decision I ever made!

Above: Writing was the ideal profession, allowing me the flexibility to visit Jennifer at whim while she was at boarding school in the UK.

Above: Outside my flat, Alexa Court, in Kensington, London, where the CIG deal was brokered.

Facing Page: With some of my earliest books on feng shui. My first book was written out longhand and sent away to be typed up! Then I decided I really needed to learn to use the computer, and I must say, knowing Word, Photoshop and inDesign is a HUGE advantage when crafting a book.

The big success of my feng shui book took me by surprise...

You cannot dig a pond inside the house when you renovate, as that would be a disaster feng shui wise.

Digging inside the house causes loss of wealth, but bringing in the pond by building walls around it so it comes indoors, that's the correct way.

Now I know that our children grow up and are gone forever. Careers on the other hand always resurface and usually in better permutations. As mine did.

I did not want to miss being there with her, for her, and my long suffering husband who had put up with my ambitions to be a big success, to make lots of money... well, after I got both, they sort of felt hollow without my family. The commuting thing with my daughter had taken its toll on her and on my husband.Yet he had somehow found the patience and the willpower to believe that one day I would indeed return. I guess I am just lucky to enjoy this kind of loving. I owed it to him and to her to return home back to them. There was really nothing to keep me in Hong Kong.

By the time I returned, our house energy had weakened terribly. It was now Period of 7. The house was still a Period 6 house so its chi vitality had dropped significantly. If we were to enjoy good feng shui here, I would have to initiate a renovation immediately.

Changing the house to Period of 7 brought about three things

Firstly, we embraced the outside fishpond, bringing it into the house, and this we did by extending the size of our living room. We brought the old garage area and the old outdoor verandah area into the home and in so doing also brought the fish pond in. Later, my Taoist feng shui friend in Hong Kong told me it was a stroke of genius what we did, for by bringing the fish pond into the house, we were creating excellent feng shui for wealth accumulation!

"You cannot dig a pond inside the house when you renovate, as that would be a disaster feng shui wise. Digging inside the house causes loss of wealth, but bringing in the pond the way you did, by building walls around it so it comes indoors rather than stay outdoors, that's the correct way." And yet of course, the decision to do so had been taken against the advice of other feng shui Masters here in Malaysia... Our good friend then, a feng shui master of some repute, Yap Cheng Hai, strenuously advised against bringing the pond indoors. He was convinced that doing so would create bad luck for us. He suggested we keep the pond outside and to use glass panels from the inside for us to "see" the pond.

But my husband and I decided that would not make good sense, so we went ahead and did it our way which was simply to build the extension around the fish pond, in effect "embracing" the pond, bringing it indoors. As it turned out, that was a very good decision and today the pond is still indoors and I have kept many generations of feng shui fish inside there.

Later, I was to come to realize that it was after we brought the pond indoors that we began to really prosper as a family, and that was also when fresh prosperity came to us. So making that decision was, with the benefit of hindsight, an extremely good decision.

Secondly, we changed the Flying Star Period for our house. To make the renovation meaningful, we changed our roof tiles and the marble in our living room floor; and then we also changed the main door. These major things we did meant that we had instantly revived the energy of the home, revitalized its chi energy and more importantly, created Period 7 energies for it.

I had to harmonize the chi of the house to that of the Period, otherwise our home would be seriously lacking in chi energy. So I invited new heaven (roof), new earth (floor) and new mankind (door) energy into the house.

Thirdly, I changed the facing direction of the house. Previously, the house had been facing Southeast 2. Now I changed it to face Southwest 2. I did this to avoid the bad numbers of the Southeast 2 Period 7 chart and I realized that by changing the facing direction of my house, the numbers in the chart worked much better, both for my husband and for me, but especially for my new profession as a writer.

At first I had hesitated, because my husband is an East group person and Southeast is his *sheng chi* direction. For me, however, Southeast was my *total loss* direction and that was the main reason I

Left: One of the first things I did when I came home to Malaysia after my long stint in Hong Kong was to revitalize the feng shui of our family home, and update the "Period" of the house. This involved serious renovating, including bringing our original outdoor fishpond indoors. On the left here is the fish pond today, alive with my "feng shui fish".

My husband and I decided to go ahead and do things our way and simply build our extension around the fish pond, in effect "embracing" the pond, bringing it indoors.

Below: 3 year old Jennifer sits on the ledge of the original fish pond. In its early days, it was inhabited by my Japanese carp.

Above: The missing SW sector of our house when it was first built was I believe a contributing factor to my relocation to Hong Kong. Here I am in one of my glamour shots at the George V in Paris. I was Chairman of Dragon Seed when this picture was taken.

had left the house for so many years. Also, when the house was first built, part of the Southwest sector was missing. This was what caused me - the woman of the house, the matriarch - to leave the house and relocate to Hong Kong. That my leaving did not become permanent reflected the power of the energy of the house to draw me back!

I felt that it was imperative I change the facing direction of the house and its main door to Southwest. Since my husband was retiring, I felt it was fine for the main door to directly benefit me, the matriarch, especially in view of the fact I was embarking on a new career as a writer! Besides, Southwest was also my *sheng chi* success direction!

To make sure my husband did not suffer any negative impact from the change of facing direction, I kept the Southeast facing door for him to use, and made it the same size as the Southwest door. Both doors continue to be in the house until today!

Flying Star luck after renovation in 1994

By changing the facing direction to Southwest 2, I successfully captured the very auspicious center combination of 1,7,4 - a parent string special combination that is incredibly lucky, and in this case, with the 1 and 4 as mountain and water star respectively, they combined to bring incredible good luck for anyone in the house engaged in the writing profession.

The number 1 as the mountain star brought excellent networking luck, while the literary star 4 as the water star indicated that I would enjoy very good money luck as a result of my writing. Here, the combination of 4 and 1 in the center of the chart was perfect to help me gain success as a writer and with the Period number 7 also in the center, the parent string combination ensured all obstacles to my success could be successfully overcome.

Meanwhile, as if to reinforce the center stars, the chart also brought the same 4 and 1 star numbers into the **facing palace** of the house. This meant that the front of the house ALSO had the 4 and 1 combination, with the 4 being the mountain star bringing literary success, while the water star was 1 bringing money luck rolling in! Hence the numbers in the new Period 7 chart were very helpful to my fast-moving writing profession!

But there was more because in the **South sector** - the part of the house that governs

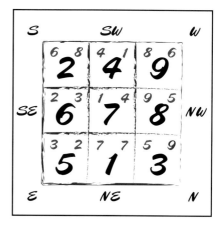

House Facing Southwest 2/3
Period 7 Chart

fame and recognition luck - the numbers were an amazing Mountain Star 6 and Water Star 8, with the water star forming a *sum-of-ten special* with the period number there.

These numbers are exceptional because they not only bring fame and fortune for us residing in the house, the Water Star 8 here also meant that fame would lead to additional wealth luck, especially if I also activated it with the physical presence of water. As for the mountain star, the number 6 brought special luck from heaven. This meant success would continue through to the end of Period 7 at least…

And then in the sitting palace was the *fabulous double 7*, with the powerfully potent number 7 being the mountain and water stars at the back of the house.

> In period 7, the number 7 was lucky, but more than that, the number 7 was also very strong & vigorous. So having the double 7 in the sitting palace was extremely lucky for the house and for us. Thus in renovating the house, we successfully revitalized it to bring us all extra good feng shui!

The new energies would last us well into the new millennium, i.e. until February 4th in the year 2004 when the Period would change to Period 8, and then it would be time to undertake another renovation if we were to continue to benefit from time dimension feng shui; but something happened in 1997 that prompted me to expand the house and hence undertake yet another renovation.

But I am getting ahead of myself. I have to put on record here that following the renovation of the house, which took place in

1994, the local feng shui books I had written and self-published for the Malaysian market just took off. They became instant bestsellers and suddenly I was visited by two major publishers from the UK.

Element Books' MD **Julia McCutcheon** and Random House commissioning editor **Judith Kendra** both flew out to Kuala Lumpur to sign me up as their author. WOW! It was quite something because both were huge names in the UK publishing industry. The **Element** book came out first and became an instant bestseller. But when the **Random** House book came out as *Essential Feng Shui*, that too became an instant bestseller. So the house renovation of 1994 that created the new Period of 7 energies brought me big success almost immediately.

Meanwhile Jennifer was blossoming in school in England. I had kept her bedroom at home well-decorated and energized with all the auspicious objects of success. And each day for at least an hour, I would turn on the fan to energize the room with movement.

I always explain to my friends that even though their children may be away at school, it is so important to keep their bedrooms at home well-energized and to make sure the chi energy inside the bedrooms never stagnates. So we kept the room clean and imbued with yang chi even though it stayed empty for ten weeks at a time.

I followed my own advice so for a couple of hours each day, I turned on the fan and the lights. The room door and windows were kept open so chi could move around. And we made sure there were plenty of photographs displayed inside the room to give it a lived-in feel. In any case, Jennifer flew home at least three times a year for her vacation break; and most years, she also returned for the week-long exeats. So even though she was away at boarding school, we saw a lot of her and the feng shui of the house was really benefiting her a great deal because the 4/1 combination, as well as benefitting me, was also benefitting her. This was because the 4 is the flying star number that brings good fortune in scholastic pursuits.

At **Benenden,** Jennifer transformed from a very average performer into a star, attaining straight A's for every subject taken for her O-levels and also straight A's in

Above: **Here I am, standing at our original SE facing door, which benefitted my husband Wan Jin. When I returned to our house, we renovated to change the house to a Period 7 home. One of the things we then did was to add a SW-facing door to benefit me, which I believe contributed much to my success as a writer. It also made the matriarch sector as prominent as the patriach sector.**

Below: **Jennifer, aged 9. She was the main reason I decided to leave the corporate world, cash out and come home from Hong Kong.**

her four A-level exams. She was offered admission to **Cambridge University** to read Economics, and when she left Benenden, she swept the Sixth Form prize for Mathematics, Economics and English - truly a clean sweep that overwhelmed me to tears. I recall her headmistress **Mrs Gillian Du Charme** leaning across to congratulate us, "It's not the feng shui," she teased, "It's just Jennifer."

Jennifer went on to enjoy Cambridge University in a way I always dreamed she would, challenged by the vigour of scholarship and truly savouring University and campus life. When we went to witness her graduation was when I felt truly thankful that I had invested so much quality time bonding with her; that I had come to my senses in time to turn my back on corporate working life in Hong Kong and focus instead on my little girl.

It was by my returning to Malaysia that I had succeeded in sending her to Benenden and from there she had made it to Cambridge... and now there she was growing up to be such a beauty and such a star. Both my husband and I were incredibly happy then, and very proud. It felt so good being parents and having that incredible moment that hung over the three of us like a vanilla sky... Oh wow!

Who cares if it was good feng shui or not that brought us to that moment. Watching our daughter graduate and then later back in London celebrating with close friends, then returning to our small apartment in Kensington, was quite magical - one of those days in our lives we will never forget.

But also at the back of our heads that burning question - would Jennifer decide to stay on in London, get a job in the City there and opt for one of those investment banking jobs in one of those fancy Wall Street firms, like her classmates, or would she come home? Everything in me wanted to scream Come home, darling! But of course the decision had to be hers... well, Jennifer decided to come home!

And of course it was the feng shui! I had kept her Southeast located bedroom so well energized, I knew deep inside me she would decide to come home. The Southeast is the direction of the eldest daughter and since she is an only child, this is the all-important direction to keep activated to benefit her. Jennifer is born in the Snake Year, so the Southeast is also her astrological location. Having her bedroom here made a great deal of feng shui sense actually!

She later told me she preferred staying in our big house at home and being spoiled by Lita our housekeeper than staying in our postage stamp of an apartment in London; and having to cook and do all the housework herself. Of course, returning home also meant she could continue her passion for her horses. The riding club she goes to is just five minutes away...

It was amazingly lucky for me, for her and for us as a family that she did decide to return home, for on coming back, she deiced to work from home. So she started a small business building websites for those keen on having an Internet presence. Those were early days for the Internet business.

Jennifer had mastered her web building skills at university and had made wonderful pocket money building her unofficial Titanic site, fueled by nothing save her love for the movie; she started selling Titanic-related products made by others from her website and discovered this was a cool way to make some pocket money. In fact, her site had become more popular than the official site, so that small success had inspired and encouraged her.

In 1999, she built the **Lillian Too website** and successfully marketed it so well that she caused a resurgence of demand for my books. She also started planning my Feng Shui Courses and marketing them from off the website - basically finding new ways to tap into the growing popularity of feng shui. It was wonderful being promoted by one's own daughter because the level of trust is both exhilarating and yes, rather soaring...

By then we had become each other's best friend! Over time, she was to evolve into my most demanding critic but also my greatest fan. I respected her command of the English language, and her simple but very sound logic, so that over time she also became my sounding board and my best editor ever. Her rationale for making strategic decisions about what books I should write, creating the angle and the treatment, gave me fresh new perspectives and insights. She also started meeting my English and American Publishers and attended the **London** and **Frankfurt Book Fairs** to learn firsthand about the book trade.

In no time at all, she was helping me decide what books we would publish ourselves under our own imprint **Konsep Books** and which to sell to overseas publishers. She helped me very much with the marketing and positioning of our books within the growing popularity of feng shui worldwide. Hers was an incredibly complimentary viewpoint to my own.

It is great being able to strategize and have real discussions with one's own daughter, and to have the level of respect that I have for her and her judgements, well honestly, this is something I really wish for everyone. I believe there is no better feng shui than this! I guess what I am feeling is pure happiness.

Spiritual Awakening
Lama Zopa Rinpoche contacts me

In 1997, I learn that my first feng shui book has attracted the attention of a very high lama – indeed, he is so taken by my book he sends me a fax, followed soon thereafter by a handwritten letter inviting me to go to Bodhgaya in India to meet with him. He also calls me by phone from Katmandu over the Chinese New Year in 1997, requesting me once again to go to India to meet him. Despite initial misgivings, I did indeed fly to India as Rinpoche had requested.

My eventual meeting with Lama Zopa and the spiritual awakening the meeting created within my mind has been adequately chronicled in *The Buddha Book* - a book I wrote several years later which was published by **HarperCollins**; here I only want to say that meeting Rinpoche completely transformed my view of everything and in the last twelve years since meeting him, my life definitely has changed forever... for the good I might add. The change did not happen instantly. It was not an overnight thing, but as I came to respect and love Rinpoche for his incredible purity, his humility and his great and flawless wisdom, I found myself embracing everything he stood for.

Rinpoche's presence in my life since that fateful February day in 1997 in Bodhgaya when I met him, recognized him and embraced him as my high lama, has transformed the way I live and the way I respond now to events that happen in my life.

Above: **Meeting Lama Zopa Rinpoche completely transformed my view of everything and in the last 12 years since meeting him, my life has definitely changed forever...**

Above: **A beautiful thangka of Green Tara - one of many in my rapidly growing collection.**

Below: **A golden Stupa, a gift from Lama Zopa Rinpoche.**

Facing Page: **With Lama Zopa Rinpoche in my garden in 1998.**

Shortly after meeting Rinpoche in India, he comes to Malaysia and stays in my home. I am certain that his presence in my home must surely have transformed it, because since then, the house has been growing - literally expanding in size and becoming increasingly more beautiful and more comfortable. The feng shui has also improved by leaps and bounds as the house metamorphosed to become the mansion it is today, where before it had been just a humble little bungalow.

I was so taken with Rinpoche that I decided I simply had to build a new wing to my home to accommodate a special room for him, one where I could house the statues and paintings of Buddha I was soon discovering.

Rinpoche presented me with the most amazingly beautiful thangka - a Tibetan religious painting - that I just fell crazily in love with. And when I took up Rinpoche's invitation later in the year to visit Katmandu to see his monastery, Kopan, nestled in the foothills of the Himalayas, I saw yet more art, iconography and paintings, that I knew I had to expand my home!

I also wanted to build an altar, so there developed an inexplicable sense of urgency within me.

In 1998 the following year, I set into motion the construction of a three-storey new extension to the front of my house. Miraculously, we got the plans approved in double-quick time and the whole construction took less than nine months. It was as if some inexplicable hand was helping me…

The extension totally transformed the house! And here's the amazing part! The new three-storey wing cost me $680,000 to build and shortly after I completed it, I was able to earn exactly that same amount of money, so of course it went into financing the whole structure! Miracle or what?

With the new extension, our property was built to the maximum. My garden was gone now and there was only a tiny strip of grass in front of my house. But the new structure now gave my house a very prominent bright hall in the Southwest; it was small but definitely a bright hall where chi energy can settle and accumulate before entering the home.

More importantly it lengthened my house, making it *five rooms deep*. This of course is very auspicious because it ensures that whatever good feng shui is done for the house will last beyond five generations, benefiting our descendents luck as well as our own. Houses are also better deep than wide! So the way we were renovating the house - making it long and deep - was correct.

Better yet, I now had a wonderful room for Rinpoche on the third floor of the new extension. It was big and beautiful with windows opening out to magnificent views of our neighborhood. So in no time at all, I had my brand new altar. I filled the walls with beautiful thangkas acquired from Katmandu. Rinpoche presented me with some more of these mouthwatering works of art and now he had also started giving me beautiful statues of various different Buddhas, explaining to me just how powerful the presence of these holy objects were. "Just by their mere presence in your home, Lillian creates skies of merit," Rinpoche always said to me each time he came to stay.

Decorating Rinpoche's room that year in 1998 created the cause for me to eventually amass the most wondrous collection of prized thangkas, statues, stupas, prayer wheels and other beautiful art pieces - holy objects that literally transformed my good feng shui house into a pure land.

This of course takes several years. The renovation that added Rinpoche's room to our home started in 1998 and was completed the following year. It led directly to the start of WOFS.com, our feng shui business.

Yes it brought an investor and it brought new capital into our life just after we activated the newly revitalized energy of the home with a wealth-bringing ritual. Soon after that… CAME THE JACKPOT! Readers who know me know that I don't just arrange my space feng shui, I also revitalize and update my feng shui each year to stay harmoniously aligned with annual changing energies… then I also undertake *feng shui*

rituals to attract mega super duper extra auspicious good fortune, especially during the fifteen days of the first waxing moon of the lunar new year.

So in the year 2000, as we entered into the new millennium, I decided that on the first day of the lunar New Year we would have five lions dancing and jumping around the entrance of the house, and then we would also have them roll big, juicy oranges to signify gold being rolled into the home. This is one of the more potent of prosperity rituals that is just so auspicious to do on the first day of Chinese New Year.

So that **Year of the Dragon** that opened the door to the new millennium, bringing us into the 21st century, was when we rolled Oh so much gold into the home!

In addition to oranges, which sound like KUM in Chinese (also the word for gold), we added ingots and real money notes. I placed nine currencies into wallets and rolled these in with the boxes and boxes of oranges. It is a sight to behold doing this, especially with five lions prancing happily and the drums and cymbals clashing away, making so much noise waking up the Earth energy - so pleasing to the "landlords", the local spirits who protect the land.

This last part is vital because every house has its own local landlord spirits who must always be kept happy and one way is by offering incense regularly. There is a special prayer and mantra that goes with this. So even as the lions are dancing, the cymbals clashing, and the drums beating, we simultaneously use charcoal to offer fragrant incense to the landlord protectors… so that was what we did that Chinese New Year of 2000, the Year of the Dragon!

It took only 6 days for the ritual to show results, for on the 6th day we got a call from one of Malaysia's most successful business tycoons, a very wealthy man who offered us the capital to start an Internet website on feng shui! When we told him that we already had a website, he offered us $15 million to buy 70% of the business.

I explained that 15 was not a lucky number for either Jennifer or me; that our lucky number was really 168, so we agreed that he would pay us $16.8 million for 70% of our feng shui Internet website business. But having a big brother partner brought in more than just money.

Above: **Each year without fail, 5 lions would dance in our house during the first day of Chinese New Year. Last year was lacking in Wood and Metal element energy, so I arranged for 4 golden lions and 1 green one to visit and dance in our house.**

Below: **My grandson Jack has a wild time arranging the oranges each Lunar New Year!**

Facing Page: **I always make it a point to have hundreds of mandarin oranges - together with ingots and coins - rolled in by the lions each Chinese New Year. This brings great abundance luck to the home for the year ahead.**

Here, Jennifer and her two boys, Jack (4 yrs) and Josh (3 months) enjoy the New Year celebrations.

Above: Our **World of Feng Shui flagship store at the MidValley Megamall.**

The new investment transformed Jennifer's fledgling online business into a solid company with big capital and we wasted no time at all, immediately expanding operations to grow the business globally.

But then something went wrong. I made the mistake of listening to my old friend Master Yap Cheng Hai when he strongly recommended that I place an aquarium in the Northwest sector of our office.

This was where the numbers were mountain star 1 and water star 6 with the period number being 8. He had got excited by the presence of the 1,6,8 auspicious white numbers and immediately concluded that a water feature there would be good. What he had overlooked was that placing water in the Northwest would seriously exhaust help coming from our mentor the tycoon.

Also we had a big aquarium here and it had somehow caused the auspicious mountain star 1 to "fall into the water" as a result of which it would cause serious staff problems.

A senior manager who had been hired to help us manage the company had been so busy politicking for position that the office had come to a standstill. So that first year was our horrible year. In the third quarter of 2000, the internet bubble collapsed with Internet companies suffering high-profile drops in their share prices. Nervous about the collapse, our tycoon decided to substantially scale down his equity in our company. We also lost some of our staff, and the company itself was bleeding expenses. In short, we were losing money fast… and with no reliable source of income in sight, things looked really grim.

I immediately did a *feng shui postmortem* and very quickly found the cause of our problems, it was the aquarium being in the wrong sector of the office.

I quickly had it dismantled and set up in another part of the office. Then I rearranged the general office furniture, tore down all the walls that had created private offices for three key managers.

I left only one private office intact, Jennifer's, and I arranged her desk to make sure she now sat facing her best personalized direction. Then I dismantled my own office to work from home. Next we appointed Jennifer the CEO and left her to reorganize the company, retrench staff and start anew.

In a year, she successfully turned the

company around. From a loss of $3 million, the company achieved break-even and by the second year of her full-time management, the company went into the black. We have been profitable ever since...

The turnaround was achieved by Jennifer creating an entirely new business model, and by me being smart enough to leave her alone. Yes, she had some help from good feng shui, but she also made some really great decisions.

Jennifer was also happy; and going through her good period, because this time corresponded to her meeting Chris, her soulmate, to her falling in love and eventually in 2002, to the two of them getting married.

Two years later, Jack, my first grandson was born and the company started to do exceptionally well. The new business model proved to be spot on... we were growing fast and expanding in new directions. I can only say what a difference good feng shui makes!

But the period is beginning to change again and by February 4th 2004, we are welcoming in the new Period of 8. Once again it is time to think of renovating the house to revitalize its Heaven, Earth and Mankind energies.

Renovation in 2004

Preparing for Period 8 was an exciting time for me. I belong to Kua 5 which is the alter ego of the number 8, so I knew that the coming period of 8 which will stretch from February 4th 2004 to 2024 would be a fulfilling twenty years for me...

Period 8 would be the period of the young man, and of the mountain. The direction that houses the Direct Spirit of the period would be Northeast, and during this time, the axis formed by the Northeast and Southwest would be key to unlocking the goodies of the period.

Our house sat on this axis. We faced Southwest and our house was sitting

Northeast, so I just knew this was going to be a good period for us. It thus became imperative for me to ensure the house was transformed into a Period 8 house as soon as the period changed. Which is why I scheduled to undertake period transformation renovations in the year 2004 itself. As soon as the New Year was over, I brought the contractor and the workmen in. What we did was change the entire roof of the house.

Opening the house to the skies was a powerful way of attracting new heaven energy.

It also gave me a chance to change to the new maroon glazed rooftiles I had been eyeing for some time. These were very good Japanese tiles that would never get discoloured, always look new and more importantly, that would reflect the sun's rays and keep the house cool.

I thought they looked very smart indeed and the effect after it was done pleased me very much. They gave the house a brand new feel which was what I was trying to achieve.

Next I had to think about changing the floor. I did not fancy having to dig up my living room; indeed, as we were staying in the house, any excessive construction taking place was sure to affect us. It was vital that we did not do too much digging and drilling INSIDE the house itself.

This would cause too much disturbance to the energy, hence causing instability... so what I did was I decided to change only the floor around the house i.e. OUTSIDE the house. My indoor floor was left intact and because there is so much "floor" outside the house, I reasoned that this would still qualify my house for the change of energy into Period 8.

As a token recognition of the change of Earth energy inside the home, I did change the marble in the foyer area and this took only a day's worth of drilling, so I decided that the house could take it.

On the outside, we dug up all the old tiles and re-did the floor with washed pebbles, a flooring that uses beautiful tiny pebbles imported from the Philippines, then laid over concrete on the floor.

The effect makes it look like granite, so it is very beautiful, except it's a lot cheaper than granite. What was great is that now I can walk barefoot and feel the earth beneath my feet. It is a good feeling; makes me feel

Whenever the Period changes, it is imperative to renovate the house to revitalize its heaven, earth & mankind energies.

Period of 8 will last until 2024 and anyone who has not yet transformed their home energy to be in sync with the new period are likely to suffer setbacks from the tired energy of their homes.

grounded and strongly connected to the earth. I laid wash pebbles over the entire outside foyer, the garage and all round the house. It looked very nice and gave the house an earthy feel.

As the Earth element is the wealth element in *my paht chee* destiny chart, I felt that the concentration of Earth energy was very beneficial for me, especially since what benefits me also benefits the rest of my family.

Then finally there was the door. It is not difficult changing the main door, except in my case, I had to order two doors, one for the Southwest-facing wall (my door) and one to face Southeast (my husband's door). I have two main doors, one facing a West group direction for me and the other facing an East group direction for my husband.

Both doors were exactly the same size, made from the same hardwood timber and carved with the same design. The SW facing door strengthened the facing direction of the house, except that this time I also shifted the angle of the door slightly, tilting it ever so slightly to now capture the SW1 direction!

I wanted the house to face SW1 in Period 8 because I wanted the Water Star 8 to be at the front - in the facing palace - where I planned to build a small and very private swimming pool. It is excellent to have water in the front of the house, especially if there is also a main door there, as this always brings growth luck. Water at the front door activates the growth chi of the house.

I had to be very careful about the exact facing direction, as the house actually faces the SW2 sub-direction, but I know that I can also use the tilted front door to basically 'flip' the flying star chart into a SW1 facing house. I can do this simply by tilting my SW facing front door. That is exactly what I did, so if you look at my door now, you will see it is tilted ever so slightly. Doing this brings the Water Star 8 to the front and the Mountain Star 8 to the back - perfect for tapping directly into the good chi flow of Period of 8. Things are sure to get better after I build my SW pool!

Right: Our home today enjoys two main doors - one for my husband and one for myself. The SW door however has taken over from our original SE door as the more significant of the two, facing the same direction as the house itself. We made this change when I was just embarking on my new career as a writer and the center numbers of 1,7,4 that resulted from this new Flying Star chart benefitted my new writing profession incredibly.

Southwest Facing Houses in Period 8

In the current Period, houses that sit or face the Northeast/Southwest axis directions have the potential to be exceptionally auspicious, especially houses that face Southwest and sit Northeast. Such houses enjoy the powerful "specials" of *parent string or sum-of-ten* combinations that promise a great deal of abundance. Houses that face the first sub-direction of Southwest enjoy three important attributes:

1. The Water Star 8 is at the front facing palace.
2. The Mountain Star 8 is at the back sitting palace.
3. The house enjoys the sum-of-ten combination between Mountain and Period Star in every sector.

These attributes not only bring excellent good fortune, but with the Water Star 8 at the front, they enable residents to simultaneously activate 3 important wealth-bringing methods just by placing a large water feature at the front of the house such as a swimming pool:

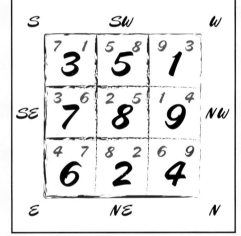

House Facing Southwest 1
Period 8 Chart (sum-of-ten)

- The pool will energize the **Water Star 8** causing wealth luck to flow inwards
- The pool will also activate the **Indirect Spirit** which is located in the Southwest in Period 8. Having water in the Southwest generates wealth luck during Period 8.
- It is always beneficial to have water in front, as this also activates the luck of **sheng chi**, which is growth and expansion luck under the Eight Mansions school of feng shui.

Apart from wealth luck, the Southwest-facing house also enjoys a couple of rather spectacular attributes that bring excellent relationship luck. Here the Flying Star chart is showing us that there is a **sum-of-ten** combination between the *mountain star* and the *period star* and this occurs in every single grid. You can see this from the chart shown above. This brings exceptional relationship luck and is conducive to generating harmony in the home between spouses, siblings and between the generations.

Then with the Mountain Star 8 at the back, this encourages residents to place a high wall to simulate the mountain at the back. Simultaneously, this also energizes the Direct Spirit of the Period which is the location of Northeast. If there is a high wall here at the back made of concrete or bricks, then the direct spirit of Period 8 comes into play bringing great popularity and plenty of excellent relationship luck.

Note: For more on the excellent feng shui of SW/NE facing houses, please see *Flying Star Feng Shui for Period 8*.

A Period 8 Pool

I used the computer to show the architect exactly how I wanted the pool to be. In the foreground of this picture, you can see my original tiny bright hall, and the tiles are marble tiles. I would change these into wash pebble to match the rest of the ground outside and then I would create a pool like this so that visually it would look as if the water was flowing inwards, bringing wealth luck. On the wall I would create a small fall of water to cause the water to move inwards also bringing prosperity luck.

I remember that when I was designing the placement of the pool way back then in 2005, it got me all excited because it would just be so perfect having water exactly right there in the SW. I knew that water in the *Indirect Spirit* sector of the period would be fabulously good. There was insufficient space to create a fancy big pool but since my pool was not so much for swimming, I felt this was quite acceptable. My pool was definitely for improving the feng shui of our house so I was not at all bothered by the smallness of the pool.

Soon after the pool got built, we successfully purchased the house next door!

This was a very BIG deal for us as I had been trying to buy this property for as long as I can remember, but somehow I never seemed to have the karma to do so. Each time the property became available at a price I could afford, the owner would change her mind at the last minute. I did expect to pay a premium for this neighbouring property of course... the owners were wealthy and successful people who were not desperate to sell and my guess was that they would not mind holding on to the property even though they had moved to a larger house in another part of town; unless of course I made them an offer they could not refuse!

My opportunity finally came in 2006 soon after my pool got built - that was when their tenants moved out and their son opted to inherit another house of theirs in Damansara Heights. The address of their house was 13 and being superstitious about this number, for years they had changed the number to 11A. (Our home was number 11.) I did not miss this tiny but significant change they made to the house number, and somehow I knew that

it was just a matter of time before the property came to us! I was right and that year they agreed to sell the property to me.

I like to think that some of the feng shui "enticements" I placed along the border fence played a positive role in their decision to let go; for instance, my giant wind chimes and the water feature I built along our dividing wall with a long spout of water falling towards my house - a very auspicious feature in any pool. In the end I think it was my SW pool at the front of the house that overcame the obstacles. And as soon as we bought the property, I set about redesigning the feng shui of my now enlarged property!

Merging the two properties

The exercise became something of a feng shui challenge, mainly because I had already so painstakingly created such excellent feng shui for our house. Now with the extra land from next door, the temptation to "extend" the house towards the right, in effect moving Northwest into the next lot was very strong. But this would have meant too many changes and the feng shui of my older property was already quite perfect... so I resisted and made the fundamental decision to keep the two houses separate. This way I would not directly affect the feng shui of our original house.

I decided to build a smaller house next door to be used as an entertaining area and a guest house, and also to create a large garden at the front. This would give me the feeling of spaciousness which I craved.

The project was also fertile ground for me to experiment with some ideas I had on some of the basic "rules" of formula feng shui. I always believed that ancient rules of feng shui need to be interpreted to suit modern contemporary living. Enhancing entrances and creating auspicious luck correctly according to facing directions are all well and good, but I also wanted to create a home that reflected my lifestyle, while harnessing the energies of lucky compass directions correctly.

So here I was with two properties, one a house we have lived in for over 30 years, and the other a new house we have just acquired. Our original home had grown steadily in size since we first moved into the neighborhood and as the house grew so our original garden had dwindled. When my first grandson was born, we knew we had to expand our living space, not so much the interiors but definitely

Enhancing entrances and creating auspicious luck correctly according to facing directions are all well and good, but I also wanted to create a home that reflected my lifestyle, while harnessing the energies of lucky compass directions correctly.

My home should be comfortable and maintaining it must not be too much trouble. It must exude happy vibrations, make us feel relaxed ...

Above: I arranged for an Infinity Pool with the infinity symbol at the bottom to activate the Indirect Spirit of the Period. To have a water feature in the place of the Indirect Spirit brings wealth luck to the home and to the residents of the home.

Right: Swimming with the grandson Jack is somehting I do quite often. He feels quite brave when he is with his Grandma!

to create more garden space, a place for them to run and romp and soak in the natural environment, feel the sunlight…

I wanted a garden that would be a bright hall, harnessing chi for our continued well being and good fortune. Somehow I had to capture the precious energy I knew would settle into the oasis of green I planned to create on the extra land that I had acquired.

But how? I knew I had to allow my home to have access to the chi being created. I had to find a way for the chi to flow into my home. So the first thing I did was to create an opening from my original house to the new garden space now alongside my home. Would this work? Can I use this side space as my bright hall? I decided that it made sense to do so.

Good energy surely can come from any direction as long as I keep it gentle and meandering. I have always maintained in any case that the practice of good feng shui should always be a logical thing; and for me it has always been about common sense and making the best of what we have… so although my garden is now not in front of the house but on the right side, I felt this would also benefit my husband, as this meant the good luck chi was coming in from the Northwest direction… good for him (because he is the Patriarch of the house) and also good for me (because NW is a very good family direction for me based on Eight Mansions!)

So I went ahead. I opened my NW wall and created an opening into my brand new garden. In doing so, I instantly transformed that precious new space into a *bright hall* for the house we used as our living space. What was great was that this new opening in the Northwest was diagonal to both my husband's door (facing SE) and to my own door (facing SW). This made the opening auspicious to both of the main doors.

Why? Because the new opening did not sit in a straight line from the main doors - being diagonal, the energy would slowly meander no matter which way it moved, thereby making the chi flow very lucky indeed!

Right: The Bright Hall in our home is not directly in front of the main house. Instead, I created the Bright Hall by its NW side, in accordance with the land's natural orientations.

It is now two years later, and I am convinced the experiment has worked beautifully for good fortune chi now settles amazingly well in the garden, then makes its way into my home through an entrance that is NOT my front door. So now I can tell you for certain that the bright hall does not have to be directly in front of your main door.

As long as chi from an open space can enter into your home it brings good fortune energy! The key is to make sure there is a doorway or opening for the chi to enter and it helps to keep this open through the day which I do!

Above: Enjoying the "bright hall" in my garden with my Golden Retrievers Jumbo and Google - these darling pets are like my personal Fu Dogs.

Below: I have always had dogs in my life. These Golden beauties joined my two Cocker Spaniels, who protect the inside of my house. My Goldens mostly roam the outside and are excellent guard dogs at night...

Pets bring fabulous yang energy into any home, especially energetic pets such as dogs. My "Goldens" also signify prosperity luck. Here they are... Jumbo & Google.

Welcoming Lucky Chi

My bright hall brings lucky chi into my home through a side entrance! To entice the chi more effectively, I built a wide patio, an outdoor living space that fringes the new opening. An extended low roof creates a shaded verandah that now looks out into a beautiful lawn in the mornings and evenings; and when the lawn transforms into a **sea of sunshine** in the afternoons, that is when maximum yang chi gets created. Believe me it is magical. The energy that arises is extremely enticing because the warmth of sun is always embracing and never harsh.

To create the ambience of peace and tranquility, mantras chanted to soft music is played continuously through the day…

In merging the two properties, I also made sure I kept the facing direction of my original house unchanged. I have a SW-facing orientation, a direction that is great for me - and I had very painstakingly created it in 2004 when Period 8 came upon us. My pool and fishponds, drains and waterways thus continue channelling good feng shui into the home.

The main doors stay the same and there is no need to change anything. Besides, now the new opening in the Northwest benefits the Patriarch, my husband, so on balance, the feng shui is very much improved. This new opening into the garden is also diagonal to his SE-facing door, the one suited to my husband because he belongs to a different Kua group

from me, so the new door really benefits him hugely. After building the access for chi to move into my home from the new property, I can then focus all my attention to creating a truly auspicious garden. This is to make sure my new "bright hall" - the place where good luck chi gathers before entering my home - would be bathed with plenty of good energy brought by the sun, the wind and the rain.

The new open space was not a pristine plot to start with; the land was uneven and lower than the level of our original house, so it had to be filled with new earth. We had to allow time for the earth to settle. This gave me the excuse to bury some **wealth-bringing coins** into the land. I tied over two thousand coins with red ribbons and buried them all over the garden to symbolically ensure

"gold in my garden". Metal energy in the earth creates the wonderfully auspicious productive cycle of the elements within the earth. Biologically, this also adds minerals and metals into the earth making it a lot more fertile! Naturally, there are few kinds of land more auspicious than fertile land. It was also necessary to build a labyrinth of underground pipes to facilitate underground water flow. This ensures the garden does not get flooded during our tropical monsoon rainy seasons, a time when the soil can get really heavy. Good drainage is definitely good feng shui as there is nothing more unlucky than clogged-up water trapped in the earth. And good drainage also ensures the lawn grows level and springy.

I tied over 2000 I-Ching coins with red ribbons and buried them all over the garden. Metal energy in the earth creates a wonderfully auspicious productive cycle of elements.

Our home today has become something of a showcase for good feng shui, although I did not set out to make it so. However, in the past eight years, we have hosted so many thousands of students to my **Master Practitioners Courses on Feng Shui** that the house sort of evolved into its role as a place for me to demonstrate how directions should be taken, how orientations are to be set in place and how the different sectors of the home are energized.

My students come from over 38 countries around the world, so they live in different kinds of houses. Many of them reside in apartments in big crowded cities, while some are fortunate enough to also live on landed property like I do, but all of them found the real life example of my house extremely useful for them to see how feng shui principles can be applied.

What I love most about my own house is that from the outside, the house looks quite lowkey… it is only after you walk through my rather ordinary looking gates that the energy of my living space starts to embrace you with warm welcoming chi energy. Everyone who steps foot in my home feels its hospitable energies and of course, that's the way it should be. A home must always be inviting, especially the public areas, so that friends and visitors keep coming, bringing big doses of rejuvenating yang chi every time they come.

This lovely group picture of one of my **Master Practitioners Course** class makes for a wonderful keepsake of fabulous shared moments. It is amazing how over a short week, everyone bonds so beautifully creating an ambiance that is truly special.

We organise lots of activities for the class, practical work that involves bringing them to different kinds of houses, and this of course includes my house as well. So here we are sitting on the doorsteps of my house 11A. Later we would write our wishes on the helium-filled balloons and then release them simultaneously into the early evening skies. The idea is to let the winds bring our wishes to the sky dragons. This is a Taoist wishfulfilling ritual that can often surprise us when we least expect it to... So I tell my students, "Be careful what you wish for your wishes just might come true faster than you imagine." This is the fun part of feng shui - there are rituals for different aspirations, for wealth, for success and for getting rid of bad luck. In my classes, I like surprising my students with unexpected tit-bits that add so much to the practice of feng shui.

Teaching What Works

What I like about the feng shui I teach is that all the methods I incorporate into the MPC are practical and easy to use. The

interpretations of the ancient formulas are adapted to modern usage. A great deal of these feng shui methodology has been successfully used in my house and when students come and visit, I am able to use examples from my home to show them exactly what I mean. This has been a big part of our success because students are then able to visualize what applied feng shui looks like. Many of them have given me valuable feedback attesting to the efficacy of certain techniques, implying some methods work better than others; that certain formulas give better results than others under certain circumstances. This really makes me happy because I know then that I have succeeded in making them think through problems of implementation, and using good sound common sense to decide which formulas to use and what objects to focus on to generate exactly the kind of energy required. By the time they leave after spending a week in Malaysia many feel a great deal more confident than whey they arrived. Seeing their satisfied and happy smiles is what then gives me a real high.

Business Partners in Feng Shui

I am happy to say that many of my students who came to study feng shui with me from 38 different countries, have become my friends and better yet, have also become my associates and partners, joining my business mandala, building on their feng shui expertise in their own city or village. Many have gone on to become very successful feng shui consultants in their own countries, respected by many for the wonderful work they do helping clients arrange their homes and offices. With them I keep very much in touch. They provide me with feedback and share lovely feng shui tales with me. Commercially they have also become inspiring success stories, building on their knowledge and developing greater expertise

with experience. I see many of them at least once a year when they return to our part of the world - to Singapore or Kuala Lumpur to attend my Extravaganza of year end updates. Our feng shui family is growing fast and we are together taking the use and application of feng shui to an increasingly widening audience ...

Above: Peter & Joanie Lung (USA). *Middle*: Viktorija (London) and Francisco (Spain). *Picture below*: Sunasee (Mauritius) Reri & Tautu (Tahiti) with Marc (Belgium).

Yang House
Growing Organically

I make sure the house has large quantities of yang chi energy because it is this that makes it auspicious and alive. The flow of chi is constant and never ending, but it is a flow that is slow rather than fast. One is greeted always by a sense of movement.

Standfans strategically located create gentle breezes through the home; and there is always the sound of running water because the oxygenators in my fish ponds create moving water through the day and night. That they are alive ensures there is plenty of organically-created growth energy. This ensures that we too will continue to grow, which is the best antidote to stagnation.

There are lights everywhere; small tea lights placed as offerings at my altars, as well as key lighting points that light up the art that hangs on the walls.

Even during the daytime, I keep some of my lights turned on; and then here and there, at specific spots, I also hang windchimes to suppress flying star afflictions or to activate metal energies. Although these "feng shui" placements are hardly noticeable, they work collectively to create a very fine yang ambience.

As a result, the chi pulsates harmoniously at all times. The house feels alive and active. And of course I let my pair of cocker spaniels run free. *Chester* and *Juno* have sensitive ears, so anytime someone is at the gate, they will bark even before the doorbell rings. More than that, they signify life and create excellent yang energy.

In the last few years, my grandsons visiting me daily are the best source of pure yang chi. They bring exquisite good feng shui to my house as nothing else can, because as any Taoist Master will tell you, young babies and boys up till the age of 8 are the best source of yang chi. They are also very good barometers of the quality of one's feng shui.

When they are relaxed and happy and laughing in your house, you know the feng shui is great. Should they cry incessantly, then you know something is wrong. In fact, in Hong Kong and Taiwan, Feng Shui Masters have been known to bring baby boys with them when checking out the feng shui of clients' houses. My eldest grandson Jack just loves running around my house and garden, and I encourage him to do so, because his shrieks of laughter are music to my ears. These days there is definitely no shortage of pure yang chi in my house, so it is no wonder my husband and I stay youthful and strong and very healthy indeed.

Chi of Eight
This is a Period 8 house which started as Period 6

One of the things I am always recommending others to do is to transform their homes to be in sync with the energy of the Period. This is because in many ways, the *time dimension* of feng shui exerts a far stronger influence on the luck and vitality of any home and its residents than the *space dimension*. Indeed, feng shui is such a dynamic practice that there is no way good feng shui can be experienced continuously if one ignores the way energy changes over time.

Feng shui divides time into periods that last 20 years; with each 20-year period being ruled by a number (from 1 to 9) and exhibiting certain characteristics. The world is currently in the Period of 8, so the number 8 rules the luck of the world! This period began February 4th 2004 and will last until February 4th 2024 - and in these twenty years, it will be Period 8 houses that will prosper, bring success to their residents and generally enjoy good feng shui.

Period 8 houses are those built after 2004 OR they are older houses that have been renovated after the start of the new Period. Renovation here requires the heaven, earth and mankind chi energy of the house to be revitalized, so any renovation must involve changing the roof, the floor and the main door. Our house was first built in 1976, in the Period of 6, so I have changed the energy of the house to stay abreast of the transforming energy of the different periods. Today it is a Period 8 house, so the feng shui of the house is up to date…

Feng shui is such a dynamic practice that there is no way good feng shui can be experienced continuously if one ignores the way energy changes over time.

It is important to update your feng shui, chcek the annual feng shui charts, move the chi, instal cures and remedies against afflictions and revitalize the energy regularly.

Facing Page: **I have these beautiful crystal infinity symbols that look like the number 8, filled with flakes of real gold; one of them displayed here with my pair of exquisite jade horses, in the center of my home.**

Welcome Water
Living in the Valley brings Lucky Water

Above: Sitting at my desk at Hong Leong, which was constructed to feng shui dimensions. Even in those early days I was using feng shui and enjoying its benefits and results.

Below: My career luck took off after I changed the flow of water that passed my front door. I attained CEO level soon after, including being given the plum job of MD of Dao Heng Bank in Hong Kong. Picture shows me with Bank Directors and the Banking Commissioner congratulating me in 1982. Note Dragon coin logo behind us.

Note the Dragon logo of the Dao Heng Bank. Here the Dragon is holding on to a coin - very auspicious!

I always prefer living in the valley to living up on the mountain top, although the best is to live mid-levels where there is a view without being at the peak where one is exposed to the elements. Our home is in the valley, on an incline, so we are well placed to receive the waters as it flows down the road towards us.

The only problems for us in the early days when we first acquired the property was that the direction of the slope, and hence the flow of water, was going in the WRONG direction for our house based on its facing direction.

According to feng shui rules on water that flow past the front of the house, such water should always flow from right to left when the house faces a *secondary* direction.

In our case, since our house is facing SW, the water must flow from right to left pass our SW facing main door!

Alas, in our case, not only were our drains flowing left to right, but more alarmingly, the outside water was flowing left to right as well, because that was how the hill sloped! This was the main reason why, when we first moved into the house in 1976 shortly after I returned from the United States armed with an **MBA** from the **Harvard Business School**, I found it so hard to land a good job.

I remember those months as being very demoralizing especially since my classmates back in the US of A were earning big bucks in fancy investment banking jobs on Wall Street. I very nearly left my husband to return to New York to work. I felt so frustrated…

But as soon as the feng shui problem was diagnosed and we built a wall to visually block out the wrong direction flow of water, and we also changed the drains at the same time, that was when everything suddenly became great again. Actually, just a couple of weeks after we built the wall (which stands till this day), that was when I landed a job with the Hong Leong group… and began a fabulously glorious and fulfilling career working for Mr. Quek. That experience really opened my eyes to the vast importance of water flows - that it is good to have water flow towards the house BUT that we must manage its direction of flow. This is really the key to good career feng shui!

South Corner brings Recognition & Success

Anyone wanting success and recognition needs to protect their South sector because this sector governs the luck of recognition. For us, the South was doubly important because the gates into the house were located in the South sector of the property.

This meant that the South was being activated everyday - each time the gates opened and closed - so it was very important that I keep that part of the outdoors neat, uncluttered and brightly lit at all times. I also had to make sure the mechanism of the gates work smoothly to ensure nothing bad happens to my reputation.

The South is a Fire element corner and it benefits when the Fire energy here is strong and flourishing, so it is imperative to have strong growing plants in this corner.

This is because Wood fuels Fire, creating it in good supply thereby ensuring the chi here stays vigourous. So here is where I grow plants with bright red flowers and here is where the lights are never turned off!

In the early days during the late Seventies and early Eighties, the South corner brought me amazingly great career luck in terms of my corporate work - that was when I attained CEO status in big corporations in Malaysia and Hong Kong.

In fact, in 1982, I took on the job of Managing Director of the **Grindlays Dao Heng Bank** in Hong Kong - an appointment that was quite rare for a woman in those days... and then in the Nineties to the present, the South has served me even better, bringing me worldwide recognition as a writer. I have thus always looked after my South sector both inside and outside the house!

Above: **I always keep the South corner of my home well energized with twinkling lights, glitter lamps, and symbols suitable for the South such as the mighty Horse and the celestial Phoenix. This brings recognition luck that leads to promotion and success. One's reputation also improves over time when the South is properly energised.**

Celestials Protect
creating a sanctuary effect

Another thing I always stress to myself and to those who ask me about feng shui is the importance of protection. Gee whiz I am a big believer of protection and my approach in doing mine or anyone else's feng shui is always to take a defensive posture first - to guard against things going wrong; putting all the safeguards in place, before energizing for any kind of specific good luck.

This is why, to me, placing the different *celestial protectors* at entrances is simply so important.

In Chinese feng shui, we have three powerful entrance protectors - Fu Dogs, Pi Yaos & Chi Lins.
These are known as celestials because they are extinct animals. They do not exist but are instead imaginary creatures believed to be heavenly guardians.

Different parts of China favour different celestials. **Beijing** and the **North of China** love their *Fu Dogs* which look like lions.

Taoist Masters always warn to be careful using these lions because they are said to be very fierce and can sometimes turn against the house they are guarding should they be placed incorrectly or should their eyes not be correctly dotted! Many of these Fu Dogs in various postures can be seen in the **Forbidden City** in Beijing.

Then there are the *Pi Yaos* (also known as Pi Xies) and these are universally loved in **Shanghai** because they not only protect, they are also a believed to be effective appeasement to one of the most powerful annual affections - the Grand Duke Jupiter also known as the Tai Sui affliction - which has the potential to bring a great deal of nasty misfortune luck. The Pi Yao also attracts wealth luck into the family so in recent years, we have seen the Pi Yao gain in popularity. My South gates are guarded by a fabulous pair of Pi Yaos.

Note that the male Pi Yao always holds a globe on the left while the female holds a baby Pi Yao and is on the right. My pair of Pi Yaos have looked after us for many years now and they are re-energized annually by a Taoist

Master who also helps me offer them a brand new red collar each new year. This is a Taoist ritual that renews their strength and vitality.

The third kind of celestial protector is the *Chi Lin* - an animal associated with the Ho Tu numbers. This is usually described as a Dragon crossed with a Horse, so it has the head of a Dragon and the body of a Horse. The Chi Lin is regarded with great affection as it not only protects but also brings excellent feng shui to any household that displays its image.

There are Fu Dogs, Pi Yaos and Chi Lins guarding every doorway and opening around my home. Many are beautiful works or art and a couple of those I have are antique coming from wealthy homes in Shanghai. I wanted some of their old energy hence went looking…

Facing Page: **One of the magnificent Fu Dogs that guard my house. I have had this particular Fu Dog for many years now, and am constantly on the lookout to collect more.**

Below: I obtained these beautiful and unusual Celestials on my travels. The top picture shows an antique Fu Dog incense burner carved of wood and finished in gold leaf, while the bottom Pi Xie is carved out of stone, suitable for the garden.

Garage Spacious
Big Area for Chi
Accumulation

There is not much space available to us at the front of the house so I was particularly grateful that I had the presence of mind to build ourselves a large garage space - enough for three cars - as this is also a good place for the chi energy to accumulate. Our garage is located in the South corner, so it is always important to keep it well-energized.

White Walls
signifying metal/gold!

The walls of my house are painted white not just because I personally love the look of a white house but also because the element of my house is Earth - it sits Northeast thereby it is an Earth element house, so here it is Earth producing Metal because white signifies Metal.

Ordinarily, this would mean Metal is exhausting Earth, but that would have been true if the relationship had been a Wood house painted red - Fire. In that element relationship, red has upward rising energy feeding on the Wood.

In our case, the Metal energy is unmoving, neither rising nor falling, and slowly being produced by the element of Earth, so painting the house white made good sense if we wanted Earth to produce gold for us. Another suitable colour would be cream or pastel yellow to reflect the Earth element, but this is a matter of personal preference and i may well change later. From an aesthetic point of view, I felt that tropical green plants looked lush and abundant against a white background.

Left: Our garage is located in the South sector, and since South governs fame and recognition luck, it is important for me as an author to keep this area spacious, clean, airy and open.

Ambience of Abundance Creating a Sense of Plenty

When you look at the pictures of my home, you will notice I can be quite an OTT (over the top) sort of person, and by this I mean that I like to create an ambience of abundance and yes, there are times when others think I overdo things, although I have to confess I never ever feel that way. I like being surrounded by many things. I like owning many things! I am not a believer of minimalism, although I do appreciate that some people love the ZEN look and the modern chrome and glass concept kind of like the plain lines and drab grays that portray this kind of decorating theme.

For me, when space looks bare, it suggests poverty, a lack of creativity and a certain kind of emptiness which I have to confess I am quite allergic to…

I love my house to look full - to have many things to engage the senses, to always feel abundant - not cluttered but abundant - suggesting a house with plenty, filled to brimming with beautiful things, meaningful possessions, sentimental displays, every corner reminding me of a story, a reason for it being there, or just so pleasingly visual it talks to me!

I also like there to be an abundance of colour, so that happiness vibes get created. I love reds and greens and yellows and blues, and I love black and I love coloured lights! Honestly I have a phobia for grey lines, the look of metal with off whites and off blacks. These give me a sense of yin. I honestly believe they cannot be good feng shui. The mood generated becomes dull and depressive, unimaginative and somber. It is not a mood I like at all.

Once I went to see the inside of a home designed just like that, in different shades of gray; floors made of gray marble, furniture was black leather and walls stark white. The owner loved it and told me it was an award-winning house. The cabinets were painted in shades of black. The staircase comprised precarious looking steps resting lightly on a fierce looking black bar. Well different strokes for different folks I guess… as long

as they are happy I thought then… and since I subscribe to the credo that if I have nothing nice to say, better say nothing, so I kept my opinions to myself.

But inside my head I felt rather sorry… their house sure looked very modern, stylish and expensive and I guess also very 'designer' but Oh what a nightmare it must be to live in… so stark, no life at all and so cold!

Alas not that I want to say "I told you so" but I was not surprised to learn that the ultra hip couple that lived there split after just three months of moving in. There were poison arrows everywhere and the furniture looked sad and lonely and terribly uncomfortable, and definitely the house had yin spirit formation written all over it… they parted company, both sides moved out. The house stayed empty for months… and slowly died! THAT is not for me!

I love houses that breathe life, that are filled with colours, music, rhythm and with all the sounds of living! An ambience of abundance… never mind if sometimes things do not match; what is important is there must be a sense of life, with **yang spirit formation** taking place continuously, and the character of the people living there must be obvious, their eccentricities and their passions stamped all over the home. Then only can a house take on life and become meaningfully auspicious for the residents!

I love houses that exude an air of abundance and plenty. Never mind if some things don't match… what is important is there must be a sense of style and comfort.

The essence of the people living there including their passions and eccentricities should also be stamped all over the home…

Above: **A bowl filled with all kinds of goodies, from faux diamonds to crystal balls, to perfume to golden ingots. Everything that symbolises something precious or meaningful to me, placed as an offering on my altar …**

Facing page: **Ingots of gold symbolize wealth, prosperity and a sense of plenty. I always have a big bowl filled to the brim with faux ingots that instantly generates this sense of plenty. I call this prosperity programming.**

Spiritual Practices Strengthen my House Feng Shui

Above: **Just outside my main entrance, I have a sizeable Stupa covered in gold leaf. This Stupa has been consecrated and inside the Stupa are thousands of mantras. Walking around the Stupa brings great merit, something many of my Buddhist friends do when they come visit!**

Below: **On the four corners of the Stupa are Buddha relics given to me by high lamas.**

Main picture: **Inlaid into the granite floor leading up to the Southwest main door are long pieces of wood that signify the ultimate yang of unbroken lines, bringing powerful heaven energy.**

The origins of feng shui go back to the **Book of Changes**, the **I Ching**, and I have always advised those who come to me for other books to refer to a really good translation of the I Ching especially for those who want to understand the philosophy of feng shui. When you understand the meanings of the trigrams and hexagrams - the broken and unbroken line symbols that lie at the heart of the I Ching and supposedly signify the wisdom of the entire Universe - then you will surely understand the theoretical basis of feng shui and its many different formulas.

I do not go very deep into the study of the I Ching but I have spent time contemplating about the meanings of the hexagrams; to an extent that I know the great value of the root 8 trigrams. These trigrams directly affect the feng shui of any space, and knowing their inner meanings and attributes enable me to use them to great benefit. The two most important trigrams are the Trigram **CHIEN** which signifies ultimate yang, symbolized by three solid unbroken lines; and the ultimate yin whose trigram is **KUN**, which is ultimate yin and comprises three broken lines.

The presence of CHIEN, the ultimate yang trigram, in any home is extremely auspicious and this is easy to make happen. Just have a series of solid lines, at least three lines in a row, one line above the other and this creates yang spirit formation something that strongly benefits the man of the house.

When there are six solid lines, it becomes a hexagram, which is a trigram doubled - and here, the concept of **double goodness** applies. So when you enter my house, you will first enter my little outdoor foyer area which serves as a mini bright hall for chi to settle. This is the small space between my SW door and the pool. Here, solid teak wood planks simulate Chien and symbolically lead the chi energy into the home. Meanings associated with Chien are all good, denoting strength, vigour and strong yang, so this is very suitable for the front of the home.

Golden Stupa blessing everyone who enters

This special golden stupa is one of my most precious possessions. It was given to me in 1998 by Lama Zopa Rinpoche who arranged for it to be shipped to me from **Nalanda Monastery** in **France**.

The Stupa is a powerful holy object which contains mantras that radiate blessings outwards, so each time we leave the house, it embraces me with protective aura, while each time we return it welcomes us back. One of the great advantages of having a

stupa like this in the home is that we can circumambulate round it each day. This brings good karmic merit to the residents and is very much in line with Tibetan feng shui advice. Prosperity activity to attract auspiciousness, according to the Tibetan masters always involve using the placement of holy objects to create good karmic merit.

Flanking the main door here at the Southwest sector of the home are my beautiful sky dancers. These welcome visitors into the home and in the opposite corners are two standing buddhas, one from the **Sukothai** area of Thailand and the other a Burmese-made Buddha from **Mandalay**.

Above the door a protective plaque with special mantras wards off bad luck and protects residents against misfortune. This plaque features the **Kalachakra symbol** of protection which dissolves obstacles that block success. On the plaque there is also a wish fulling mantra.

I have other similar plaques hung above many of my frequently used doors in the home, as they bless whoever walks through the doors. This plaque ensures no one is able to bring bad energy into the home. These are examples of how I have systematically incorporated Spirtual practices to strengthen my house feng shui.

More than 30 Years living here...

Top: **My husband Wan Jin with Baby Jennifer.**
Middle: **Celebrating Jennifer's 1st birthday in our then very humble home.**
Bottom: **Jennifer aged 9.**
Far Right: **Jennifer marries Chris; this picture taken during the picking up of the bride ceremony in our house.**

Jennifer was born here in 1977, the Year of the Snake, Period of 6. This was one of the most joyous events in our life! After our marriage in 1968, my husband and I had lived in a house in **Bukit Tunku**, a very posh suburb of **Kuala Lumpur** where his employers, the **National Electricity Board** had beautiful living quarters offered to their engineers.

Our two bedroom house there sat on an acre of land and we liked it there very much. But it had some serious feng shui flaws not least a big casuarina tree that directly faced the main entrance door, which itself was made of glass. Then the staircase also directly faced the door. As a result of these afflictions, our marriage was very unfulfilled because no matter how hard we tried, we just could NOT conceive...

My husband decided then to buy our own house, while I decided to give myself a break by going to the **Harvard Business School**... and in the two years while I was at Business School in America, my husband built our house in Pantai Hills - and it is here, in 1977, a year after I returned, that Jennifer was born.

Her arrival changed many things for us – the new house must surely have been auspicious, because nothing indicates good feng shui more than a *hei* event, a happiness occasion; and Jennifer's arrival was a double happiness occasion of the most magnificent kind!

Our daughter's growing up years reflected the happy years of the house's Period of 6 energy. At that time, the house was still very small. Ours had been a very tight budget and we had bought as big a piece of land as we could afford – around 9000 sq feet. But the house we built was relatively small, although at that time it was considered quite respectable at about 2,100 sq feet of built up area. What we had done was to bring in the feng shui man to arrange things such that we would have a baby. That had been the most important brief, because we were desperate for a child.

In fact, it was the success of our feng shui project to have a child in this new house which strengthened my belief in feng shui then. We had been trying for so long – nearly ten years – without success, and then to have it happen so quickly and seemingly so easily really blew my mind... so at that time, the house was very much focused on our little family unit.

Another major milestone that took place in the house was Jennifer's marriage to Chris in the Year of the Horse in 2002. The Horse is Jennifer's peach blossom animal, bringing love and marriage, so it was very auspicious indeed that her marriage luck ripened for her that year.

What pleased me no end was that Chris Yeo, her husband to be, was a Dragon... my secret friend and my husband's ally. It was a perfect choice astrologically, because the Dragon and the Snake creates the *House of Magic* together; so we welcomed Chris into the family with open arms. Having this **double happiness event** at the home revitalizes the energy of the home very strongly and in fact, every home gets a shot of precious energy each time there is a double happiness event in the home.

In the Chinese tradition, there are three events that are regarded as double happiness – a birth, a wedding and a birthday for the old family patriarch and matriarch – the older the better! So when we reach the age of 89, we will have a big birthday bash here! Jennifer's marriage in 2002 was at the tail end of Period 7, so it was really good for the house, because by then the vigour of all period 7 houses were losing steam and we were thinking of getting ready for the changeover to Period 8. These days we are strongly into Period 8 and it is another phase of our life now because we have become Grandfather and Grandmother.

We now have two grandsons and they visit us daily bringing pure energy into the home each time they come. The sound of children's voices is very auspicious and confirms the quality of the energy of our home...

Ours is a family home that rings daily with laughter. This is what good feng shui is all about and we are living with good feng shui. In the following pages, I will share ideas, tips and suggestions with you - things I did in my house that worked so brilliantly at different stages of my life, and the timeline of events as they unfolded correspond to the way the chi energy flowed as well. So the story of anyone's house is really the story of their life...

Timeline: History of this House

1976 Wan Jin builds the house for me. It is completed in the Year of the Dragon. As you will see, the Dragon plays a very significant role in my life. In every Dragon year, good things happen for me. And the Dragon itself is a symbol that brings me noticeable good fortune.

Like now, my being so actively engaged in feng shui work, surely this is the cosmic breath of the Dragon manifesting perfectly in my life... so in my house, you will see many images of the mighty Dragon. Wan Jin built the house during the two years when I was studying in Boston USA...

When I return from Harvard, **I get pregnant**. The house is auspicious! That same Dragon Year when I return home from the USA is also the year we conceived Jennifer. The Dragon creates big magic in my life!

1977 Jennifer is born. The house is in its Period of 6 (1964 -1984). In the **Year of the Snake**, Jennifer's arrival brings unsurpassed happiness to both of us.

1978 My career takes off after wall is built to block wrong flow of water. In 1978 I got a job working directly with the big boss of the **Hong Leong Group**.

He was taking his small companies public then and I was the right person at the right time for him, so I got very heavily involved in his corporate restructuring work – and that was way before the bull markets of the eighties and nineties, so you can say we were pioneers then, laying the groundwork for the Group to eventually become the multibillion dollar group it eventually became.

A couple of examples. I worked with Quek on restructuring two of his listed vehicles. One was **Sovran Industries**, which then had a paid-up capital of 5 million Ringgit comprised of 5 million one dollar shares. We pumped in his small leasing and finance companies, aggressively expanded the branch networks of these financial companies and transformed Sovran into **Hong Leong Credit** creating the vehicle for it to eventually become his financial arm. In later years, he was to add a bank and other ventures into the company and by then, the market capitalization of the company had soared into the stratospheric billions!

We did the same thing to another little listed company, **Fancy Tile Works** – at that time all it had was this tiny little manufacturing operation making floor tiles. Once again, we modernized the set up, bought new machinery from Italy and diversified into other tiles, then added a whole lot of other manufacturing operations, turning the company into the giant **Hong Leong Industries**... so this company too has a market capitalization that is in the billions.

In the course of doing all this corporate restructuring, Quek's wealth doubled and doubled and doubled, because he is such a great market operator. So we also went shopping for companies. When I worked for him then, we bought two mega-sized companies. We bought **Hume Industries** for which I arranged the multimillion dollar loans for him from **Wardley** in Hong Kong; and then we also bought the **Dao Heng Bank** in Hong Kong.

In fact, that was how I came to become a banker. Quek appointed me to the Board of Hume and made me Managing Director of the Dao Heng Bank in Hong Kong.

And all this took place in a space of four years from 1978 to 1982. Those were glory days – when I was at the height of my corporate career. My house must have been bringing me really good feng shui, although at that time I was just too busy to notice...

1982 **I relocate to Hong Kong.** When I was offered the job of Managing Director and CEO of

Dao Heng Bank in 1982, it never occurred to me not to accept, even though the appointment required me to live in Hong Kong. The move came as a shock to my husband of course, but gee whiz it was the chance of a lifetime... especially in those days, for a woman to scale the heights and shatter the glass ceiling this way.

Of course it made me so very excited. It was big news in the corporate scene in Malaysia and Hong Kong and I was on cloud nine – not a good place to be and now many years later looking back to that year, I am today surprised at my own courage of those days.

It never occurred to me to be afraid. I never doubted I could handle the job. Failure was something I never thought about – I was that kind of person! I lived my life day to day, aggressively, fiercely, strongly expecting only to succeed.

I guess that kind of positive belief in oneself must have been what had propelled me into such a high profile big responsibility job; because even by today's standards, it was a very BIG job... and it really said a lot about my boss then – his courage to entrust me with his new billion dollar investment for that's what the bank had cost him – a cool billion dollars!

How did I do in my new role as Bank CEO in one of the world's largest financial capitals? Not badly at all I have to say! Those were heady days, so busy, with no private life – when there were simply not enough hours in a day... but this is not a book about my career.

Suffice to say, those years running the bank really opened my eyes to many "practices" amongst financiers which eventually led to the rise of the hedge fund Gods and the warriors of Wall Street... and eventually to the subprime mortgage debacle that led to the global crisis. The global financial meltdown in 2008 is many years later and I am so happy I am completely out of that line of work and now doing something wonderful like feng shui – really helping people improve their energy and attract good fortune into their lives...

1984 **The Start of Period 7.** Two years after I left for Hong Kong came Period 7. A change of period always brings traumatic change and for Hong Kong, it coincided with the rise in anxiety over its reverting back to China. **Maggie Thatcher** the British PM came to visit Hong Kong and her visit brought the issue of the 1997 when Hong Kong becomes part of China into sharp focus. Those were troubling times for the people there, many of whom used this period to relocate out of Hong Kong. Made me realize how lucky I was to be a Malaysian!

1988 **I return home to Malaysia.** I realized around the mid-Eighties that Hong Kong was a place for me to increase my net worth, make my fortune and go back home. To do that alas I would have to part company with Quek. It was not an easy decision. I wanted to send Jennifer to private school in England and for that I needed to be seriously rich, not just be an employee no matter how grand sounding my job was. I had a great job with the **Hong Leong Group** and no one could have wished for a better boss or a better work environment than the one I had... and the money truly was not bad. But if I stayed on, I would always be an employee. No way I could make the kind of millions I wanted. I had got used to the rich lifestyle...

More importantly, my *paht chee* chart was telling me that that was the right time of my life to think about becoming wealthy. If I missed that period, it would be a shame. I knew I had to somehow package some kind of deal, then turn it around and make serious capital gains.

I quit my job, joined up with my then best friend, fellow banker **Cynthia Picazo** and together we packaged a leveraged buyout of the **Dragon Seed** department store, which involved us borrowing to the hilt. We leveraged the whole amount! We did the deal in 3 months, then went into the company and within a year had successfully turned the company around, easily tripling sales turnover and profitability, and more importantly, Cynthia and I brought back glamour to the store and made it an exciting place to shop.

Within 18 months, we persuaded our equity investors to cash out and take profit by selling the store with its newly minted image. The move to sell had been prompted by my growing urge to become a full time mother.

Both Cynthia and I had wanted to shop like Empresses, hence we had chosen to buy and manage a department store – we both loved shopping – and we had thought being the chief buyers for Dragon Seed would make us blissed out on shopping. The reality had been completely different.

A year of buying from trade fairs, attending zillions of fashion shows, ordering thousands of pairs of shoes... it sort of paled on us both very quickly and we decided then that banking was a whole lot easier and more cost effective. So it was easy for me to persuade her that just as we had packaged a deal in, now we needed to package a deal out.

We sold Dragon Seed for a fat profit; everyone was happy. We divided the proceeds and I returned home. The deal had made me and Cynthia into multi millionaires! It was wonderful... now I had more than enough money to retire forever!

I also had more than enough money to send Jennifer to private school. I sold everything I had in Hong Kong, my business, my investments, my apartments, my cars, and booked a one-way ticket home!

1989 After I return from Hong Kong we holiday in Pangkor. Back home in Malaysia we became once again a family. Jennifer was ecstatic I was home and I immediately made plans for us to go to England to find her a school. We took a trip to England then, the three of us, and visited several schools, and happily, when it was put to the vote, the decision was unanimous. The three of us loved **Benenden** and we especially liked the headmistress **Mrs Gillian Du Charme**.

We returned home to prepare Jennifer for the entrance exams. I spent three months giving her private coaching in Maths and English and happily she made it. Benenden accepted her as a student for the coming new term. It was now summer and she would start school in September.

We meet up with the turtle on the beach... a sign of things to come!

That summer prior to Jennifer going to boarding school in England, we went for a family vacation to Pangkor Island. That was the time when a big 'turtle' swam up to us by the beach. It had strange markings on its back and at first we thought it was alive, but when we got close enough to examine it, turned out it was actually just a turtle shell. But it had looked very real.

It was following that encounter some years later that I started writing the feng shui books that would open a whole new career and life for me. At that time, I did not make the connection, but years later I did, because the source of all feng shui formulas is the **Lo Shu Magic Square** which had been brought by a turtle to the legendary **Emperor Fu Hsi**. That turtle had been a sign of things to come; it had in effect been an oracle, only at that time, I did not know... The big surprise is that we even took pictures of our holiday in Pangkor. Above is a picture of Wan Jin and Jennifer looking at the turtle shell that came in with the tide.

1990 I live in London for a year, Jennifer is in Benenden. I did not want Jennifer to feel I had returned from Hong Kong only to abandon her in England, so I bought an apartment in London and parked myself there for a year – just to be near Jennifer. I also wanted to "lose myself" in London, soak up the art and the culture of this great city. I had always wanted to live in London, feel its pulse, soak up the special flavour of this great city.

That time of my life seemed a perfect time to do it. I was tired of working life. I wanted only to visit museums, art galleries, hop over to Paris, bond with old friends and just do nothing. It was quite a perfect time, because I had no responsibilities then save to be a full time mother. And don't forget I was sitting on a pile of cash… so all I had to do was manage it.

That year in London was magical… but as Jennifer got used to boarding school, I got bored of doing nothing and living alone, so once again, I returned home to my house in Malaysia.

1994 House Renovation to tap the energy of Period 7.
In any case, I had this nagging thought then that there was something I had to do – and that was to transform the energy of our home to that of the new Period of 7. When I came home from Hong Kong, I had been appalled at the low stagnating energy of the home. So I decided to fly back to Kuala Lumpur from London and get this important project organized.

We embrace the pond, bring it indoors - start of our wealth period. We brought our outdoors fish pond into the house, by building around it expanding the house quite considerably. I remember after we did that was when we as a family really started our wealth period together, because by then I had the capital to make investments and build a new business . Till today we still have that beautiful pond and it has seen several generations and different kinds of fish …

1995 Feng Shui Books take off…
I wrote my first book on Feng Shui in 1995. Unexpectedly, the book took off. In three months, I had sold ten thousand copies, so I reprinted and that was followed by yet another reprint and another and another. So I came out with my second book, and my third book , and soon it seems that feng

shui has taken over my life. Today I am still spreading the wonderful skill of feng shui and am convinced more than ever how important it is for everyone to know at least something about this living skill.

As of now I have written over a hundred books, but of course this is counting the 12 astrology books I write each year on the 12 animal signs with Jennifer…

1997 Meeting Lama Zopa Rinpoche; Good Karma Ripens.
One of the most memorable meetings I had after I had renovated my home to change it to Period 7 was meeting Lama Zopa Rinpoche – a high lama of the Tibetan Buddhist tradition. Meeting him changed the way I looked at life and it's been incredible the impact Rinpoche's teachings have had on my mind and my attitude. That meeting took place in February 1997 in Bodhgaya in India.

His presence in my life also brought real meaning to my existence. I feel really inspired that I can use my knowledge, experience and whatever skills I have to be of benefit to people. That kind of transformational energy is awesome, and I can only describe it as the ripening of good karma.

The CIG becomes an International Bestseller!

In the fall of that same year my internationally published book **The Complete Illustrated Guide To Feng Shui** hit the number 1 spot in the Barnes and Nobles list of summer bestsellers. This was a very big deal as B and N's bookstores in the USA really publicized my book hugely across America. I honestly believe that Rinpoche's wonderful blessings had a lot to do with my success with the book.

1998 House Renovation to build room for Rinpoche.
I have to confess that my reaction to meeting Lama Zopa in 1997 drove me to chase Him all over the world. I kept flying to wherever he was to attend his teachings and to learn from him. That was a

very intensive time and when he also came to my home to stay with us… I felt really bad that I did not have a special visitor's room to place at his disposal.

I did however rearranged my own bedroom and offered it to Rinpoche. But after that visit I decided I really liked the idea of having a High Lama come visit me… and that was when I started another renovation, this time to build a three-level extension that would have the top floor made into a penthouse room for Rinpoche…

This is how the front of my house came to eventually lose its garden and I added 3 floors of additional built up area to my home. This expanded my house considerably, so it was now well over 6000 sq ft in size.

2000 **New Millennium. WOFS gets established**… money rolls in! Shortly after the front extension was built, Rinpoche came to stay the following year and the year again after that. This corresponded to a time of great spiritual growth for me and by then Jennifer had come home and was busy building her fledgling website business. As for me, I was spending a great deal of time following Rinpoche around the world.

The Period of 7 is generally considered a magical time, a period when there is a flowering of interest in esoteric knowledge and all things metaphysical. Globally, interest in feng shui as well as in Tibetan Buddhism reached an all-time high.

By the year 2000, interest in feng shui had peaked to such an extent that my books had become incredibly popular. That year on the 6th day of the lunar new year was when some super duper money rolled into our home – some millions of dollars of investment money that was offered to us to start WOFS.com as an internet business to popularize feng shui online. Jennifer's website on me and my books was thus converted into a portal site on feng shui …

She had been working off her laptop in her Southeast bedroom then and it truly was like a dream come true when she was offered $16.8 million for 70 % of her WOFS.com website. With that kind of money invested into her company we started to grow the company. Definitely the house MUST have exceptionally good prosperity luck – literally the money was just rolling in…

2002 **Jennifer Gets Married – Double Happiness Occasion!** Jennifer's romance with Chris culminated in a spectacular wedding. It was wonderful seeing them so happy. Chris was at Architectural Graduate School in the USA when he first met Jennifer so they conducted a long-distance romance at first, but he soon came home to marry her, agreeing to live in Malaysia and building her the most beautiful house ever – just two doors away from mine.

Their marriage in 2002 was a terrific double happiness event that reaffirmed the excellent feng shui of our house; that was in the Year of the Horse – Jennifer's peach blossom animal!

2004 **Jack is Born. Another Hei Occasion! Monkey Year!** Happily and without too much prompting or trying, Jack our first grandson arrived two years later. Needless to say, this double happiness event sent us all over the moon. Jack being a Monkey is Jennifer's secret friend and is Chris's and Wan Jin's ally (Dragon, Rat and Monkey make up the Ambition driven Trinity of the Zodiac). Jack's Monkey is also my Rooster's commercial ally… so astrologically the combinations were perfect.

2004 **House Renovation to transform my house into a Period of 8 house.** That year starts a new feng shui period, so we had to renovate the house again, this time to bring it in line with the new chi energy of Period 8. Changing the roof and floor tiles was the big thing of this renovation – vital revitalization of heaven and earth energy.

2005 **Build the Southwest Pool to tap Water Star 8; Rooster Year.** With the new Period 8 chart in place and my house nicely tilted to face SW1 its time to build the Southwest pool which also activates the Indirect spirit … I built a pool which had water visually flowing towards the home!

2006 **Acquire 11A - Build Guest House. HOUSE EXPANDS!** I succeed to buy the neighbour – at last and instantly, I expand the house, creating a new bright hall which is sure to massively improve our feng shui. And now we have the garden I have always wanted! This makes a great playground area for our grandchildren to run, ride their bikes and host playdates for their friends.

2008 **Josh is born – another rejoicing Hei occasion! Rat Year!** Two years after we expand the house and four years after Jack we have yet another grandson. Truly our cup runneth over.

As a Rat-born in October, Josh has great similarities with his maternal grandfather (see picture above!) Since then my house rings daily with the happy laughter of the two boys who, being Zodiac allies get along beautifully. The next grandchild is being planned for the Year of the Dragon i.e. 2012!

Above: **The three boys in Jennifer's life are astrological allies. Chris my son-in-law is a Dragon, Jack my 1st grandson is a Monkey, and Josh, my 2nd grandson is a Rat! Yes, it was planned that way!!!**

Left: **Baby Josh with my husband Wan Jin, who makes an extemely proud and doting Grandpa!**

The Dragon in my life...

We are a very happy family and every one of us in the family benefits hugely from the presence of the Dragons in my home...

Writing this book made me realize how significant the Dragon has been in my life. When I look back at all the Dragon years for instance they were years that have marked vitally important and auspicious events. Almost always, it seems those years were when significantly important events happened. I also discovered that the actual kind of good luck that came in each of the Dragon years had a direct correlation with the meaning of the elements in my life destiny paht chee chart...

CONSIDER

1964 - In the **WOOD DRAGON** year when I was 18 years old, I sat for my Sixth Form 'A' level exams and that was the year I surprised myself and my Mum and Dad as well by scoring 4A's which means I got As in all four subjects I sat for. I also won a Federal scholarship to University – hey, that was a BIG deal for us! In this Dragon Year, I was living in **Dragon Temple Lane** in Butterworth!

1976 - In the year of the **FIRE DRAGON** when I was 30 years old was when I graduated from the **Harvard Business School** in the United States with an MBA. Oh boy, that too was a very big deal. My two years spent at business school really brought me some spectacular career advances … and has been a boon to me all my life. The Fire element represents creativity and intelligence for me. In this Dragon Year, I was living in Boston USA.

The significant job I landed two years after I came home from Harvard was with the **Hong Leong Group**, whose logo was also the Dragon. It was at Hong Leong that I learnt the most about how to do business and how to survive the corporate rat race. Hong Leong was where I developed my corporate strengths. When I was with them, I made sure the Dragon logo was given prominence. Some years after I left them, I think when their old patriarchs passed away, they decided to go for a more modern look, so they designed a new corporate logo.

1988 - In the year of the **EARTH DRAGON** when I was 42 years, the year brought me **Dragon Seed** department store, my leveraged buyout deal that made me RICH and enabled me to become truly independent ...when we cashed out after making a meaningful profit on the deal, I decided to retire from corporate life and return home to Malaysia. The Earth element stands for wealth luck in my destiny chart, so it was definately a very meaningful year for me. In this Dragon year, I was living in Hong Kong...

2000 - In the year of **METAL DRAGON**, I am 54 years old and that is the year we set up WOFS after seed money comes in via a prominent investor who decides to bank roll the setting up of our world of feng shui publishing, wholesaling and retailing company. The Metal element signifies influence and power in the chart and I guess establishing WOFS to sell branded feng shui using my name falls into this category.

Whatever it is, the 2000 Dragon brought wonderful new directions into my life, having WOFS and doing all the things we have been doing since its establishment – writing and publishing our books and doing the Extravaganza Updates each year and the feng shui courses – these activities of mine have not only been amazingly fun; more important they have been incredibly fulfilling. This is the only Dragon year when I am living in my house in Malaysia

2012 - The next Dragon Year will be in 2012 and it will be the year of the **WATER DRAGON**. What's coming then? Perhaps a third grandchild... well, Water stands for my resources in the Paht Chee chart, so it is really the best element for me. So hopefully what comes is something excitingly spiritual. I am convinced I have something great to look forward to. Hopefully I shall still be living here when 2012 comes around...

PART 1
ENTRANCES

The entrances of homes are usually the most highly energized space because people walking in and out of the house activates the chi here. As such, the feng shui at entrance areas including foyers just inside and outside entrances must benefit from good feng shui features. This means that attention must be paid to the orientation of doors which must be correctly measured and positioned to benefit residents. Attention must also be given to protective symbols placed here to guard the home. These should be annually refreshed at the start of each new year to ensure that chi energy entering the home is always auspicious and always full of vigour.

You can have as many entrances as you wish, and in fact, the more you have the greater will be the inward flowing chi.

Different residents can use their own favourite entrance to take advantage of their their favourable directions based on Eight Mansions feng shui. However the most important entrance is the main door. When there is good feng shui here, good fortune enters the home with ease.

My house has many entrances facing different directions but the main two correspond to my, and my husband's best directions of SW and SE respectively.

WELCOME WORLD
my guest entrance is wide & welcoming

It is excellent feng shui to have an 'open house' or party once a year. Such events attract plenty of yang chi into the home.

The sound of human voices and music is what attracts cosmic energy from the Universe and this makes the home come alive.

This is the entrance that plays host to visitors. It has been made wide and welcoming so that anyone invited to my home can feel the warmth of our welcome… the steps and different levels were not created for feng shui reasons but to accommodate the different levels of the land.

The view of my home as you walk the three steps up to my garden is the wide walking space which I eventually transform into a **Corridor of Buddhas**. This is where I display several of my modern day art deco pieces and a few beautiful **Mandalay Buddhas** from **Burma**. Here, trees, plants and shrubs grow lush and pleasing, creating a lovely area that is shaded from the sun, yet is still outdoors enough to enjoy our sunny tropical weather.

This "corridor" was designed to be wide so that this part of the house can serve as a "cocktail" area for guests to mingle, admire my Japanese carp in a large pond here, and bond during the lunar new year. That is when I normally hold an Open House dinner party. This is very much a Malaysian tradition that is observed also by the *Muslims during Hari Raya* and the *Indians during Deepavali* - and is one of the great attractions of living in Malaysia.

Many people host Open Houses in their homes during their respective festive seasons and this is when every kind of truly yummy local food is served at standalone "stalls" in gardens across the city. Guests come between certain prescribed hours so the host has a chance to interact with all the guests who show up. I usually invite my guests to come at different time slots; this ensures that the whole auspicious day gets imbued with plenty of good vibrations.

It is excellent feng shui to have an 'event' like this once a year - such events attract copious amounts of yang chi into the home; the sound of human voices and music is what attracts cosmic chi energy from the Universe and this makes the home come alive.

It is important to invite only people whose outlook is positive towards you and whose goodwill towards you is obvious. It is better feng shui to be surrounded by good feeling friends than have a big crowd that comprise of people whose feelings towards

you are tinged with even the slightest bit of negativity… this is what brings discordant notes into homes, and such notes can fester and grow strong, eventually manifesting as obstacles and aggravations. Remember that cosmic energy - negative or positive - never dies; instead it always grows stronger.

It is vital that discordant notes are dissolved in the days following any party that takes place in your home; especially when you serve anything alcoholic…

An easy way to purify negative energy is with an incense offering to "local protectors". These are the **Spirit Landlords** that live alongside you in your home and they will efficiently sweep away any lingering negativities if you appease them with incense and smoke offerings.

New Year parties are excellent for yang chi formation and when there is a continuous stream of people entering the home bringing gifts, flowers, red packets, and other auspicious offerings, these attract excellent luck into the home.

During the lunar New Year, people traditionally exchange gifts with each other. Homes get cleaned and are then decorated with auspicious decorative objects and symbols, and it is really beneficial to use this time of goodwill to create good vibes. The Chinese believe that when the first fifteen days of the year's first moon is spent happy and contented, the rest of the year will follow likewise.

It is also a good idea to invite guests into the home throughout the year as this is what ensures the energy stays uplifted and high.

Visitors can bring positive impact into any space, especially when they come bearing gifts. I am blessed with many good friends who always bring goodies every time they come and visit and I am definitely very appreciative of their good wishes as it transforms into good feng shui!

Above & Left: Me and a few old friends enjoying an auspicious first day of new year morning at my home during one Chinese New Year. It is always auspicious to have a full table of food spread out to signify abundance, and to only invite friends who bring genuine good cheer and make you feel great about yourself. Four of my friends pictured here with me have been my pals for well over thirty years. Three of them, from right, Shahreen, Mariam and Siew Yong were at University with me. Aishah is a freind from my Hong Leong days while Winnie and Cindy are friends from my feng shui decade.

Above: The Taoist Eight Immortals sit atop my "relationship wall" in the SW of the adjoining property.

Activating Mountain Star 8
Flyover brings good Feng Shui

Lucky mountain stars usually bring excellent relationship & health luck to residents. Since I am using this second house for parties & entertaining, it could not have been more appropriate that the house is so significantly dominated by the strong Mountain Star 8.

Facing Page: The flyover highway and payment funnel visible from my garden acts like a symbolic funnel for wealth to flow continuously into my home!

One of the more important feng shui aspects of my house is that because I have kept the two properties that make up my home separate, there are two houses whose respective feng shui is arranged separately. So I treat them as two houses with *different Tai Chi*. This actually makes it a lot easier to design the feng shui of the home.

When I renovated the second property to merge with my original house, we cut the built-up area of the new property into half, leaving only two bedrooms to serve as guestrooms and a large living area for entertaining. This idea was very attractive because the house here faced SW2 - so the Water and Mountain star numbers of this house are exactly the reverse of my original house. There the house faces SW1, while here, the house is facing SW2.

What this means is that the **Water Star 8** for the guest house flies to the back and the **Mountain Star 8** flies to the front - exactly the opposite of the other house. This was incredibly lucky because within view from the front of the new "guest" house, about 200 yards away, is a huge highway! This multi-level highway looks very big indeed

from where we live. Thankfully though, it does not look hostile or appear in any way threatening. In fact, it can be regarded as the auspicious **mountain** that activates my **Mountain Star 8 at the front**! So I set about tapping the powerful feng shui of the highway.

This **elevated highway** is a recent addition to my neighbourhood, and when I investigate its effect on my home using the Yin and Yang Pa Kua formula, I discover that the highway is actually auspicious for our house. We had at first been rather worried; but it has been some years since the highway was built, and it has proven to be good for us.

I liked the **feng shui symbolism** of every passing car dropping a payment into the payment funnel. The toll gate happens to be directly visible from our house! This seems like incredible good feng shui. Thankfully, it is not a very popular highway, so it never gets noisy, but the "money" dropped into its till also does not get to be very big either!

Great Relationship Wall

Lucky mountain stars in the Flying Star chart usually bring excellent relationship and health luck to residents, especially when they are correctly energized. In our case, we already had the elevated highway to activate the mountain star, but because I

am a very *kiasu* person (*i.e. an exaggerated perfectionist whose attitude is always to do things twice so as not to lose out*) I decided also to raise the wall here, making it higher than it was originally. From the outside, the wall looks high indeed, but on the inside, it is is only 5 feet high.

The wall gives us precious privacy, and more, it signifies excellent feng shui as it is very much in sync with the auspicious Mountain Star 8 here. Since I am using this house for networking and entertaining, and as a guest house for foreign friends visiting me, it could not have been more appropriate that the house is so significantly dominated by the strong Mountain Star 8.

A year after the wall was raised and lovely trees planted to create a private sanctuary effect, I also placed the **Taoist Eight Immortals** on the wall. These created a beautiful ambience and made the wall even more powerful. The presence of the 8 Immortals always brings good feng shui into any household and I am pleased to say that in my home I have at least three sets. This being the Period of 8, having the 8 powerful Taoist personalities is exceptionally meaningful.

Raised Elevated Gardens

The spacious garden in front of the wall is slightly raised, but is on the same level as the original house. Here is where cosmic chi from the great outdoors accumulates and settles before making its way into both the houses. This garden is truly special as it is here that **heaven energy** from above – from the blue skies and the great night skies – settles and then makes its way into my home.

All the doors and openings into my home that face this garden are never closed as I want to entice the chi energy to make its way into the home itself. I definitely think of my garden as being very auspicious; it has large amounts of sunlight as well as shade, yang and yin… it has beautiful trees and lovely flowering plants – all of which grow sturdy and lush. This itself is an indication of good feng shui. And it has a feeling of space because the grass grows flat and green, creating a magnificent lawn, a sea of green.

Here is where I play with my **American Goldens**, retrievers who are as big as lions and equally as beautiful… they are young and frisky and playful and my grandson Jack loves playing hide-and-seek with them.

Chi-Accumulating Hall

My garden area is frequently washed by a gentle breeze which causes the leaves to rustle, making me very aware of the beautiful tall trees that have grown so fast and so tall here.

It is really a great boon to be able to enjoy a **bright hall effect** in one's home – as this is said to be central to tapping into the cosmic energy of the Universe. Nothing brings better feng shui than a clean and fresh bright hall that gets regularly rejuvenated by the winds, the rains and the sunlight.

In my garden, we have all these in varying degrees of intensity. There are days when the breeze is truly gentle as it kisses your cheeks and other days when the wind becomes a roar, howling frighteningly across the tree tops. Then I can almost feel the ferocity of the skies…

It is the same with the rain; usually there will be a slight drizzle in the early mornings or late evenings, and these are wonderful as they quench the thirst of the plants. But there are other times when the rain becomes a tropical monsoon, and then the drains outside fill with a fierce raging river-like flow that could easily sweep away everything in its path. Here in Malaysia, the rain can become very scary indeed.

And then there is the sunlight which can be so gentle you feel like lifting your face up to the sun and have it bathe your cheeks with colour. There are days when it gets so burning hot that even walking the wash pebble ground becomes like walking on hot coal… these are the days when my **Cocker Spaniels** simply love taking a sunbath, so they sit in the sun allowing the magic of sunlight to warm their skins and make their hair shine with golden brilliance!

Herein lies the incredible range of the energy of my home – something I would not change for anything in the world, because the greater the intensity of the natural forces of wind, rain and sunlight, the deeper is the great good fortune these forces bring! And no matter the intensity of the chi energy that settles in the bright hall, it accumulates and it will make its way into my home…

Above: **Because the patios in the home are so wide, they double up as chi-accumulating bright halls.**

Below: **My big lucky willow tree captures the soft embracing breezes that flow into the property.**

Facing page: **My cocker spaniels Juno and Chester love to sunbathe in the verandah area between the two properties. This sleepy lady here is Juno and she has been with me now 8 years.**

Main Entrance
at House Number 11

House number 11 is my original home. The number 11 is extremely lucky for me because I was born on the 11th January and according to Taoist Feng Shui Masters, the number of your day of birth when repeated as a house number brings the good fortune of "double goodness".

And so it has been. In fact, I often think that it was when my neighbour on the right changed her house number to 11A (from 13 which she believed to be unlucky) that it would only be a matter of time before the house became mine. That was probably how I came to successfully buy it after lusting after it for many years!

The entrance to number 11 is located at the South sector of the home, so the opening and closing of the gate here daily activates a sector which traditionally brings recognition. Here is where I make sure the lights are kept brightly lit, the flowers planted here are red in colour, and the gate itself is wide and welcoming.

The garage placed here is likewise large, big enough to fill three cars; it was designed to be like this to ensure it is big enough for any amount of incoming chi to feel welcome, settle in and accumulate.

When there is a wide enough space just outside the doors of the home, then only can good amounts of chi accumulate successfully before it enters the home through doorways and windows. The idea is to create a feeling of spaciousness rather than have cramped, narrow spaces.

I made certain that there would be no bedrooms built directly above the garage, as I believe it to be bad feng shui for anyone to sleep above an empty space. The garage is part of the extension I built in 1998 when I created a three-level new wing to the house, prompted by a desire to build a very special room for my lama. This creates the cause for Rinpooche to visit me often.

Main picture: **Skydancers flank the main front door.**

Prime Space
The Importance of Entrance Feng Shui

An important characteristic of the main door is that it should be large, and it should open into a house that has depth. This brings long lasting good feng shui.

Above: **The solid lines leading up to my SW entrance signify powerful heaven energy.**

Main picture: **Here I am standing in the foyer area of our home, just inside both of our main doors. The SE door is behind me and the SW door is open.**

As someone very into feng shui, I am extremely mindful of the importance of the entrance areas, and especially the main door area. My approach to feng shui is rather more contemporary than traditional; so it has to be adapted to take account of my living condition and my lifestyle. Thus because my husband and I need separate facing direction doors, I had to design an entrance area that would seamlessly accommodate this without it looking awkward or making it difficult for the chi flow to enter into the home.

The large garage is just one aspect orf the feng shui of my entrance area; I also had to make sure that there were two doors, one facing **Southeast** to captures my husband's *sheng chi* direction, and the other facing **Southwest** which is my own *sheng chi* direction. In front of both doors, I create their own external foyer area – for chi to accumulate. This way, the feng shui of both entrances are adequately taken care of.

The important thing to remember is that neither door should feel cramped; and both doors should be of the same size.

This emphasizes the equality of the Patriarchal and Matriarchal force of my house. However, in terms of the house facing direction, this has been designed for it to be facing Southwest and sitting Northeast. In facing Southwest, the house benefits the career and success luck of the Matriarch. This reflects the fact that I continue working still, pursuing my career as a writer, hence earning income for the household. My husband on the other hand is nicely retired, being nearly ten years older than me, so we designed a less energetic feng shui for him.

Chien Trigram

Directly in front of the SW-facing door (the door which benefits me) I have placed a series of solid straight lines that are the symbols of the **Chien trigram.** This strongly benefits the father or patriarch. The presence of this hexagram here has great feng shui

significance, as this is a powerful yang energy symbol. **Chien** does not only signify the Patriarch, it also stands for the leader and more importantly, it signifies heaven energy.

So with this powerful symbol of heaven here in the SW, which is the place of Earth energy, what is powerfully created is the presence of heaven and earth, the two forces which when combined with our own mankind energy gives us the powerful presence of **tien, ti ren** at the entrance of the house. In feng shui, there is really nothing

more auspicious than **tien ti ren**. This is a very powerful feature which not only ensures growth for the family but also safeguards the family's wealth and descendants luck, two important attributes of good feng shui.

In China today, where feng shui is seeing a major resurgence, you will find that in cities like Shanghai and Beijing, those places with names like *Sin Tien Ti* – which means new heaven and earth will always signify centers of good feng shui. Malls named this way also signify places with good feng shui!

Another important characteristic of the entrance is that it should open into a deep house. My house is five rooms deep and this ensures that good fortune can last for at least 5 generations. Already I have 4 generations in my family, counting my mother, me and my husband, my daughter and her husband and children, and this of course suggests good feng shui. It is always better to have a house that has depth rather than breadth; the deeper the house, the longer auspicious feng shui can last, and as a rule of thumb, it is good to have a house that is at least three rooms deep!

Happily Southwest

Today, the facing palace of my home is placed in the SW and the main door here also faces SW. As we are currently in the Period of 8, this is extremely auspicious. This is because in the current period, the SW/NE axis brings amazing feng shui. This means the house is sitting NE and facing SW.

The Northeast is described as the Direct Spirit of Period 8 because in the original Lo Shu square, the number 8 is the number of the Northeast. When the Direct Spirit of your home has a *mountain* to activate it, it brings extremely beneficial relationship and socializing luck.

Above: **The space between the door and the water is where good cosmic energy accumulates.**

If you activate the Direct Spirit of the Period with a "mountain", people are well disposed towards you, and members of the family are harmonious with each other. You will have plenty of friends and will not suffer from gossip or politicking. Health will also be excellent for residents living in the home.

It is even better if the Flying Star chart also has the Mountain Star 8 at the back of the house, as this strengthens the effect of having higher land behind - exactly the way my home is configured. I have higher land behind me and am in fact supported by a symbolic **tortoise mountain**.

What I have is land that slopes upwards, and there is even a big house behind supporting my home. That house belongs to a very wealthy man, so being supported by such a magnificent house at the back brings excellent support for my SW-facing home. Even better is that behind that house is yet higher ground, ensuring there is plenty of support for my home, and so it has brought me good feng shui all these years.

Indirect Spirit
Prosperity through Period of 8

To ensure that my **Mountain Star 8** is indeed at the back of my house, I tilted my front main door slightly to ensure that my house faces the direction of Southwest 1.

I took directions many times to ensure this, because not only did I want the **Mountain Star 8** to be at the back of my house, it was also very vital for me that the **Water Star 8** in the Flying Star chart of my house is located at the front of my house! See the chart here.

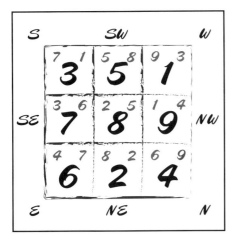

This brings a double benefit of having water at the front. With Southwest being the place of the **Indirect Spirit** of this current period of 8, if I have water in the Southwest, it would effectively activate wealth luck for the home. This is because the Indirect Spirit always brings wealth luck when it is energized by the presence of physical water!

This is one of the most powerful indicators of prosperity luck in the Flying Star system of feng shui, and even when your Southwest is not at the front of the house, merely placing a water feature in the Southwest of your apartment or a pond in the Southwest of your garden will activate excellent prosperity luck.

For me, having the Indirect Spirit at the front of my house (because this is the Southwest sector) helps me to get multiple benefits from the pool that I eventually built there.

Above: **A clear view of the number 8 mosaic-ed onto the bottom of our infinity pool. 8 is always a lucky number in feng shui, and especially in the Period of 8, the current period we are living through now!**

The Indirect Spirit always brings wealth luck when it is activated by the presence of water.

Water Star 8
Luck of Asset Accumulation

It is vital to change the energies of your home to those of the current period if you have not already done so. Updating the energies will give your home a new lease of life and prevent chi stagnation.

With the house now facing Southwest 1, I know that for the twenty years from 2004 to 2024, my house is ruled by the Flying Star chart which places the **Water Star 8** at the facing palace in front and the **Mountain Star 8** at the sitting palace at the back.

Below are the Flying Star charts that apply to my house in both the preceding period 7 and the current period of 8.

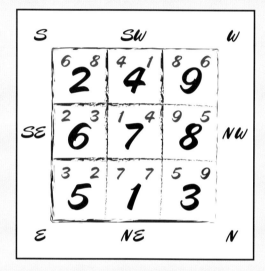

Flying Star chart of our house in Period 7 prior to renovation to change to Period 8.

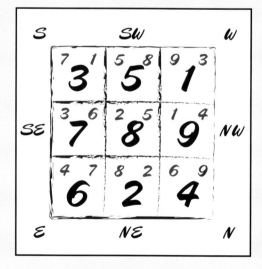

The current Flying Star chart that applies to our home today.

The house is presently enjoying the chi vibrations of the Period 8 chart because I transformed it into a Period 8 house in 2004 as soon as the period energies changed.

This is something I have been strenuously advising many people to do. Unless you have just moved into a brand new Period 8 house, chances are that you are staying in a Period 7 house. If so, you are likely suffering from **stagnating energy** if you have not yet changed your house into a Period 8 house. The chi in your home needs revitalizing.

Also, in many Period 7 houses, the number 7 is at the facing or sitting palace, and this means that the ill effects of the number 7 – which brings violence and robbery – will hurt residents.

The number 7 was very lucky during the Period of 7 but now that the period has changed, the number 7 has turned ugly and reverted to its true self.

In Period 7, my house was facing SW2 and if I had not changed my house into a Period 8 house, I would be suffering from having a double 7 in my house's sitting palace and that would have been extremely harmful for all of us living here. You can compare the Period 7 and Period 8 charts of my house shown here.

For Period 8, I changed the facing direction of my house to make it face SW1, because I wanted to bring the **Water Star 8** to the front of the house. This would have the Water Star 8 coinciding with the energy of the **Indirect Spirit** of the period.

By doing so, I knew that then, creating a special pool of water here would be enormously beneficial! It would be worthwhile spending the money to build a pool here to activate not just the Water Star 8 which brings prosperity, but also the **Indirect Spirit** to simultaneously activate wealth luck. Awesome !

This **double benefit** is of great significance to our continued good fortune. If you look at the Period 8 chart, you will see that the **Water Star 8** is at the front and the **Mountain Star 8** is at the back of my house.

Earth Mother
Excellent for Woman of the House

What is also important is that the **Southwest** is the place of the mother energy, and this is signified by the **Kun trigram** that belongs to the Southwest. Kun is known as the ultimate Yin trigram and it signifies nurturing matriarchal energy.

When the Southwest is so well energized and when it is the main direction of the home, this strongly benefits the mother, and it also means that mother energy dominates the home making it excellent for me.

This is probably the cause behind my heartwarmingly close realtionship with my daughter and to my son-in-law and to my grandchildren Jack and Josh – so close that I see them on a daily basis! They respond to the mother energy of my home and are always keen to come to Grandma's home.

For me, this is truly excellent feng shui. It makes me feel real good that I have the opportunity to enjoy my grand children, especially when I see friends and relatives whose children now live far away in another country making it so difficult for them to see their loved ones as regularly as I do.

My extended family, comprising my brother Phillip and my other late brother's children – my nephew Han Jin and my niece Honey – with their families, are just as close to me. I play the role of the Matriarch to my extended family and it is a great feeling knowing they genuinely love me as much as Jennifer does.

Benefitting the mother energy also brings plenty of good fortune to my work, making it possible for me at my age to continue feeling relevant. For me, this represents the best kind of luck that feng shui can bring.

Top: **I take so much joy mothering my daughter and her boys and the matriarchal chi energy of my house is so strong that I find myself playing "Mother" also to my niece and nephew... here I am carrying William, eldest boy of Honey, my niece.**

Middle: **Han Jin, my nephew, with his wife Audrey and son Dominic.**

Bottom: **Jennifer with her second son Joshy.**

Main picture: One of my pair of Skydancers, which flank my Southwest-facing main door. Skydancers are believed to bring the warm breath of guardian dakinis into homes. Their presence is what creates the invisible and intangible energies that ensure good health and happiness for residents. In the foreground is one of my brass phoenixes on which skydancers are believed to fly.

Facing Page: Kuan Kung with Nine Dragons decorating his robes stands guard in an annex on the left of my SW facing door. This Kuan Kung is made of brass and his wrathful expression is believed to be sufficient to scare away any one harbouring naughty intentions. Thus he prevents anyone with bad intentions from gaining entry into the home.

Sheng Chi Rising
Water in front nourishes high growth energy

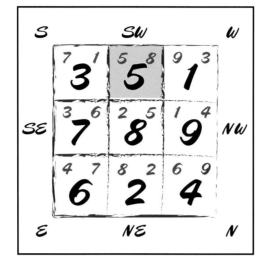

What is extremely significant is that water at the front of any house is ALWAYS beneficial. For anyone, irrespective of your facing direction, when there is the presence of physical water, this nourishes the special **sheng chi** or growth energy that resides at the front of the house.

This is based on the **Eight Mansions** formula of feng shui which maintains that the auspicious growth energy known as sheng chi always resides at the facing palace. The formula also describes this energy as **Wood element energy** which benefits from, and is strengthened by, the presence of physical water.

It is for this reason that many feng shui masters in the old days would advise their clients to have water at the front, facing their main door. This is especially beneficial for those living on landed property. If you are living in an apartment, then an **aquarium** here is very beneficial.

For me and my family, the pool of water at the front of the house thus activates not one, not two, but three significant and important prosperity enhancers. The beautiful pool that I built here is one of the most outstanding feng shui features of my front entrance area… but more on this wonderful pool, and the importance of water to bring wealth luck, in a later chapter.

Sky Dancers
Sacred Energy from Cosmic Protectors

Flanking my SW door are two lifesize **Sky Dancers** and these beautiful wooden carved statues symbolize the powerful sacred energy of cosmic protectors – Buddhist angels, if you like. I got this stunning pair from Cambodia where there are beautiful legends of sky dancers showering blessings onto earth.

This resonates strongly with my keen interest in the *dakinis*, flying angels of the Tibetan Buddhist pantheon of deities, and I place them flanking my door to indicate that all people with good intentions are warmly welcome into my home. I am also very taken with the intricacy of the wooden carvings and suspect that these works were likely done by craftsmen from the northern Thai border region. These sky dancers are thus not antique pieces.

9 Dragon Kuan Kung
Hidden Guardian Dragons

In an annex on the left hand side facing the main SW door, I have placed a Nine Dragon Kuan Kung – this is the Taoist general of the Three Kingdom period who today has become a very popular Taoist deity, respected as the God of War and also as the God of Wealth. Kuan Kong is reputed to be an excellent symbolic patron for those in business, especially those having to face the unfair competitive practices of others. Interestingly, it has been told to me that Kuan Kung is revered by both the Triads and the Police alike in Hong Kong

Kuan Kung with Nine Dragons decorating the robes on his body is considered a particularly fierce and wrathful manifestation of this popular deity. Placed here he stands guard at the entrance to ensure that all who enter the home will be well disposed towards us. Displayed this way, Kuan Kung becomes a Protector, although despite his wrathful countenance, he is also a benevolent deity. For me, I selected the Nine Dragons Kuan Kung because I have a great affinity with Dragons - the Dragon is my secret friend. Through my life, it has been during Dragon years that significant events happen for me that take me to new levels of awareness and attainment.

White Umbrella Goddess
Protects us from Bad People

On the right wall facing Southwest, I have placed a very beautiful thangka of the **White Umbrella Goddess**. This is a powerful **Buddha of Protection** who carries a white umbrella that has the power to symbolically dispel any evil intentions of people who may want to hurt us. I am always mindful of this possibility and believe that one cannot be too careful about always having protection against those who might wish to harm us…

In fact, all people whose work puts them in the public eye - corporate figures and politicians, or people who are prominently successful in some field or other - tend to be vulnerable to the jealous intentions of unscrupulous people, enemies or competitors, so it is better to be safe than to be sorry.

In my own life, I have intermittently encountered people who have attempted to cast black spells on me, as a result of which I am now very mindful of underlying currents of jealousy.

The White Umbrella Goddess has a thousand hands and is said to be the wrathful protective emanation of the **Compassionate Buddha**. She protects in a benevolent manner, dispelling bad intentions by transforming evil motivations into harmless ones. This is why I like her very much indeed and regularly recite her mantra to ensure she is "present" in my home. Below is her powerful mantra:

Above: A lovely thangka of the powerful White Umbrella Goddess, which I commissioned from Katmandu hangs on the right side wall beside my SW main entrance. As you can see from the enlargement of the thangka on the next page, This Goddess protects from many types of bad people and evil spirits. Note the different manifestations of forms and animals that she stands on , indicating her power to subdue them. She has a thousand hands and a thousand white parasols that give shelter to all who invoke her protection by reciitng her mantra daily.

Tadyatha Om Anale Anale
Khasame Khasame Bhaire Bhaire
Sume Sume Sarva Buddha
Adhishthana Adhishtite Soha

Om Sarva Tathagata
Ushnisha Sitata Patre
Hum Peh
Hum Mama Hum Ne Soha

(recite the last line 108 times each day)

Trunk Up
Unwanted Intruders

Anyone visiting me will be mildly amused by the number of different protectors and celestial guardians I have in my home. This in no way reflects any kind of paranoia about security... rather, it manifests my subconscious desire to protect the energy of my home at different levels and dimensions of consciousness.

Elephants have always been associated with qualities I admire – tenacity, strength and a gentleness of gait despite their huge size. Maybe that is why they are regarded as sacred animals revered by the Thais and the Indians.

In Buddhist art, the elephant frequently appears as one of the Four Friends, the others being the Bird, the Monkey and the Rabbit; the elephant also illustrates the nature of the mind as it goes through a series of transformations in its quest to attain the state of "calm abiding" and thereon to enlightenment.

As a serious practitioner of Buddhist meditative practices, I find the elephant particularly inspiring, so all round my home I display beautiful carved pieces collected from my pilgrimage travels or given to me by students and friends.

Elephants with their trunks up signify their role as door guardians, protecting the home from petty burglars and shielding residents from getting cheated.

Those with their trunks down signify the procreation of descendents so that in symbolic feng shui, this is what is recommended for those who want sons in the family to carry on the family name. Elephants displayed this way signify fertility and descendents luck. Placing this kind of elephant just outside the bedroom flanking the bedroom door is believed to help couples wanting children to conceive.

Above: This magnificent jade elephant is one of a pair given to me three years ago by Ireen, our WOFS business associate in Thailand. Ireen has been my student now for nearly ten years and she has become increasingly successful explaining feng shui to a Thai audience. The jade here is nephrite jade and the pair is so heavy it requires three men to lift each of these elephants! Jade elephants are believed to bring plenty of growth luck.

Above: I am particularly fond of these sandalwood elephants which I picked up from the holy city of Varanasi in 2008 when I went to attend a talk given by HH the Dalai Lama. When we featured these elephants on the September 2009 cover of FENG SHUI WORLD magazine, the issue became one of our highest selling issues. The carving here reflects the exquisite craftsmanship of the Benares craftsmen of India and sandalwood is of course regarded as a holy wood.

Facing Page: Golden elephants are very auspicious as they convey an excellent aura of prosperity vibrations. This elephant here with its trunk down is a benevolent elephant that I associate with the offering elephants found in temples.

Rhino Watch
Makes Home
invisible to Intruders

Placing a double horned rhino near your front door or gate is an excellent way to nullify any ill effects from the number 7 burglary star.

Above: **A brass double horned rhinoceros with intricate carvings stands watch facing the main gate into the property.**

One of the more negative of stars in the annual feng shui flying star chart is the number 7 star, which is known to bring violence, burglary and armed robbery. Obviously when one's front door is in some way afflicted by this negative star in the annual feng shui chart, and this is further compounded by the presence of the illness star in your house chart, then it is important to have the **Rhino cure**.

This is the image of the double-horned Rhinoceros, which can be done in brass or in blue coloured resin, and placed where the annual number 7 star flies to in your house. So each new year, both the Rhino and the location gets updated to make the cure truly effective i.e. to guard against burglary taking place.

For many people, reading flying star charts can seem too technical and difficult, although in truth, it is quite easy; but many people seem to have a mental block against reading charts, especially charts filled with nothing but numbers.

This was the major rationale that prompted me to organize a New Year event each year, to invite readers to spend a Sunday with me so I can explain Annual Updates in feng shui and astrology for them.

In the eight years I have been doing this, response in terms of attendance has grown terrifically each year. These days, my **Feng Shui Extravaganzas** in Singapore, Kuala Lumpur and in the United States (alternating between LA, Hawaii and Las Vegas) have become must-attend events for feng shui enthusiasts.

Pair of Phoenix
Bearers of Good News

Flanking the matriarchal door are a pair of very special brass phoenix, beautifully made and imported from China several years ago and given to me as Chinese New Year gift by a close business associate.

As I am born in the year and hour of the Rooster, a pair of phoenix is particularly appropriate for me. The Phoenix and Rooster belong to the family of winged creatures whose presence in the home, especially near the entrance, always brings good fortune.

When they arrived at my home however, I decided that merely placing them here by my door was not sufficient. I decided that to gain maximum benefit from them, they should also have their eyes spiritually opened.

This requires a Taoist ritual done by a Taoist Master or his disciple, who knows how to symbolically "open the eyes" of the phoenix and then to imbue them with the spirit of this divine bird.

Doing so activates their chi energy, making them extremely powerful. This way, my pair of imperial birds is sure to attract wonderful opportunities, and bring continuing good news for me. And this of course they have done; magnificently I may add!

These divine celestial birds also exude excellent guardian energy, so there is also an element of protective aura generated by their presence. Their size alone can be rather intimidating!

Currently, I am toying with the idea of gold leafing them to transform them into Golden Phoenixes which will then bring them into the realm of the celestials. The Phoenix is of course the heavenly manifestation of the Rooster, which belongs to the Metal element, and gold is the ultimate metal. Gold leafing is a time consuming undertaking and I have yet to get round to doing it… it's a big job, but gold leafing these phoenixes would make them even more powerful.

Above: **One of the pair of phoenixes that flank my front door. The phoenix is regarded as the King of Birds, bringing good news and fabulous opportunities.**

Above: **A small window placed next to my main door allows us to check who is outside. This is good feng shui way to dissolve oncoming chi that hits your house too fast.**

Window View
Peeping Glances precedes Door Opening

On the right hand wall of the front foyer, I have placed a small window. This is one of the secret Taoist methods of feng shui shared with my by an old Taoist Master when I worked in Hong Kong. He explained that whenever there is an unobtrusive window next to the main door where residents can take peeping glances at whoever may be visiting signifies a symbolic alert system which benefits the household. The window thus allows us to view any outside visitor before opening the main door. It is however important to ensure the window stays low key and not obvious. Mine is hardly noticeable as I have placed big plants to camouflage its presence.

Note that having a window next to the main door is also an excellent way of dissolving oncoming chi that hits at your house too fast – as when you directly face a straight road, or if you live at the end of a *cul de sac*. The window effectively slows down the chi energy before it can enter the home and this causes it to lose whatever negative energy it may be carrying.

Doors Well Guarded
Plenty of Feng Shui Protection

All my entrances and doors are well protected. This is because I believe that the best way to practice feng shui is to take a defensive posture before trying to use this living skill to get rich or successful. When misfortune befalls, one has no time to think of trying to get ahead. More important then is to ensure survival, to get well when illness strikes, and to recover when loss is sustained through whatever happens.

When I speak of protection, I refer not only to being guarded against petty thieves and burglars, or being mugged and accosted on lonely streets during night time hours. No, protection also suggests being guarded against the entrée of bad chi that results in obstacles, failures, aggravations and all sorts of reversals to one's normal good luck.

When misfortune strikes, it is totally unpleasant, and when it attacks us unexpectedly, we may not always be in the frame of mind to take good defensive action. So the Chinese have always adopted the principle of prevention rather than cure… and hence all entrances into the home should best be guarded by celestial, feng shui and even divine protection. Only then can you truly call your home a sanctuary, a place you can feel safe and at ease, free from the cares of the world outside.

So it is a good idea then to ensure that every door enjoys some kind of feng shui protection. Anyone visiting me will be struck by the number of doors and entrances I have. Indeed I like living the open space concept, so my doors are almost always open. That is the way the house has been designed, to bring the wonderful tropical outdoors in, so chi moves freely but benevolently through the home.

But every entrance is well protected, so all round the home are obvious and not so obvious "protectors" – beautiful Pi Yaos, Chi Lins, Dragons, Elephants, even Camels and Fu Dogs. I also keep lovely golden coloured dogs – Cocker Spaniels and Golden Retrievers – who symbolize the spirit essence of protector dogs.

In any case, there is nothing much to steal from my house, so it is not the material things that I am guarding. The most precious objects in my home are my holy statues of Buddha. What I am guarding really is my good energy. I make very sure negative energy has no chance of entering my home, so it is this that I guard with serious effort, and it is the preservation of good energy that becomes the essence of my defensive feng shui.

Above: **The mirror above surrounded by mantras and supported by a pair of dragons provide protection along with the other "protectors" in my home.**

Door Amulets
Powerful Mantras Confer Blessings

Door amulets & other special mantras decorate the doorways and walls of my home, conferring blessings and providing protection.

Above: **The Eight Immortals sit atop a ledge above the door that opens to the main garden area. These Taoist Saints attract good things for the residents of any home which has their presence.**

The most vital dimension of chi energy protection is that I have powerful mantras and door amulets that are placed flanking my doors and also above my entrances, which create good fortune for all who enter and all who leave my house.

The mantras confer vital blessings so that everyone who enters my home feels welcome. There is a great sense of goodwill that permeates the air. This feeling is usually created between me and all who come and visit me. I am not surprised by this expanding feeling of warmth exuding outwards and inwards, mainly because in recent years the house is becoming increasingly blessed.

This is the result of my Dharma knowledge increasing and more importantly, it is due to the invisible but very powerful and pervasive influence of my guru's advice. In the years that I have embraced Lama Zopa Rinpoche as my lama, he has shared some incredible and profound teachings about the enhancement of space and consciousness, which I have systematically implemented and incorporated into my feng shui practice.

As a result, all round my home can be seen many instances of specific advice given to me by Rinpoche. This has rarely been called feng shui and indeed Rinpoche always says, "this brings good karma" or "doing this brings great merit" but I know that when karma is good and positive and when one gains positive merit, the result is always good karma, and good karma always brings great good feng shui! Good karma also dispels all misfortunes and bad feng shui!

So above my doors, lining my overhead beams, blocking my protruding corners, flanking all my entrances and decorating my glass pane windows are various mantras, holy objects and sacred symbols of good fortune and protection.

It is from knowing about the power of sacred Buddhist icons that I eventually came to realize and understand the immense power of symbols. The eight Buddhist symbols, premier amongst which is the mystical knot, are wonderfully uplifting placed in any space or to enhance any private aura fields.

Once I achieved these important breakthrough realizations, I have not looked back and the efficacy of my feng shui practice has become better, bringing faster and more dramatic results. It is these results that I have endeavoured to share with my readers and students these past ten years! And I am thrilled to say that they have served them as well as they served me and my family.

Open plan Auspicious
Breaking down Walls expands feeling of Space

Prior to changing my home energy to Period 8, I had already been thinking through my plan to introduce the open plan concept into my living areas. My idea was to enhance the feeling of spaciousness by doing away with walls and increasing the number of "openings" which in effect would bring the outdoors indoors.

So the first thing I did was to get rid of many of the old constricting walls in my home. This instantly generated a bigger and continuous living space. The side effect was that we were immediately forced to clear out all visual clutter and to reduce redundant furniture. Clearing the clutter was wonderful for my living area, and the wider spaces that resulted took on a meandering flow which enhanced the feng shui of my home.

> The great advantage of the open space concept is that it allows me to change the "look" of my welcoming foyer space and my living area any time I feel like doing so – and this I have repeatedly done.

In fact, I move my furniture around so much, and add and subtract little pieces so often that my family has grown accustomed to the dynamics of constant change.

Above: TsaTsas are minitature images of Buddha and other deities that are made of plaster of Paris. In my home we have thousands of tsa tsa images which we make ourselves and which we stick on to walls and structural ledges near the ceilings. Tsa tsas are holy objects that radiate the blssing power of the Buddhas. I was taught how to make these tsa tsa by two monks from Nalanda Moanstery in France which also supplies the rubber moulds. Visitors to my home often gasp in amazement when they suddenly see my ts a tsas and then realise there are so many "Buddhas" in my home...

Above: **I have configured the rooms in my house and arranged furniture so that when you sit in the living hall, you can see out "as far as the eye can see". This brings good fortune from near and far and is one of the benefits of living high on mountain sides. As my house is in a valley I make sure to also look to the skies upwards to get this benefit.**

Each year, I like to add at least one piece of new furniture into my home to symbolically add to the family's accumulated asset wealth.

It is in fact excellent feng shui to ensure that the energy of one's living space is never allowed to stagnate. So each time I bring a new piece of furniture home, or invite a new decorative object into the home, I almost always have to make some changes. I also move my furniture around each time I get hit by the blues; or when I feel that life is getting a little blah. This always revitalizes the mood at home because it keeps the chi moving!

Meanwhile, each year I add at least one new piece of furniture as this is said to symbolically add to the family's accumulated wealth. I also retire one piece of furniture as this too is auspicious to do. According to the Taoist masters, it is this that keeps the ambience of the home rejuvenated and this that guards against energy getting heavy and tired. The home benefits from regular bouts of revitalized energy and it is this that ensures the ambience stays happy, light and positive. This is what in turn attracts auspicious energy and good feng shui!

Chi Accumulates
Mini Bright Hall inside allows lucky chi to settle

Open plan living is the best way to make the most of the cosmic flow of chi in the current period of 8. So I tried to create as large an open space as I could to encourage incoming chi to accumulate. My living area was built to give me freedom for multi-dimensional usage and allocation of this space. Over the recent few years, I have greatly indulged myself; redecorating and rearranging my space as frequently as I wished.

Whatever I do with the furniture however, irrespective of how I move them around, good chi successfully accumulates here. This is because in this front area of my home, what I have is the unencumbered single space concept. There are no walls blocking and impeding the flow of chi, so the excellent flying star numbers near the entrance of my home easily overflows, seeping into other corners and moving to other parts of the home. Since Period 8 charts have the luckiest numbers in the center grids, opening up the space ensures these good luck numbers also benefit other corners of the home. Literally then, chi gathers and circulates, benefiting the whole house. And because there are many open doors/entrances, external cosmic chi mingles with internally generated intangible chi to create an auspicious ambience at all times.

Those wanting to change their living areas into the single open space concept, please note that this can involve high impact structural alterations OR it can be just a simple rearrangement of furniture and corners requiring the demolition of perhaps one wall, or enlarging one doorway or window.

If you plan a radical transformation, it can involve removing several walls or even a whole floor to increase horizontal as well as vertical space. When new double height space gets created, chi energy gets released and expanded in a most wonderful way. Not only can it spread over a larger area, it also gets enhanced.

You can make your windows bigger, your ceilings higher and your outdoors brought indoors. All this requires shifts of energy that can bring great benefits because what happens is that the whole space gets re-energized. There is sure to be a new feeling of openness that improves the yang quality of your space. Magically, the spirit of the residents is certain to get uplifted. The new feeling of spaciousness is sure to bring new quality to your thinking, new confidence to your attitudes and greater value to your spatial feng shui.

Open plan living subscribes to the view that it is not necessary to separate domestic activities into separate rooms, closed in by walls. This impedes the flow of chi and can "lock up" good energy into pockets of confined space. So now, instead of following restrictive layout planning, you can do everything in one big space. Furniture can be arranged to create activity zones, making everything within reach. Awareness of and benefits from the flow of energy become

extra positive. Chi can flow unimpeded from zone to zone.

As a result, there is greater potential for creativity, resourcefulness and inventiveness. You could well find, as I did, that you become less bound by conventional straight jacket approach to doing things. In doing away with walls and demarcations, one symbolically pulls down obstacles to creative thinking.

Facing Water
Activating the Sheng Chi of the House

My main door, the one that faces Southwest, directly faces a pool of water. This activates the *sheng chi* sector of the house, bringing growth luck. The universal rule of feng shui is that the front door and front part of the house always benefits from water, irrespective of facing direction.

By water here, we mean an accumulation or body of water, and this is different from a flow of water. This means asset wealth accumulation then becomes likely for the family. A flow of water usually means income, a regular flow of money coming for sustenance. In a modern context, this generally refers to a steady income flow like a monthly salary, or regularly receiving dividends or other forms of income such as income from a trust fund.

In addition to facing a body of water, my front door also faces a small drain that has been built for the water to flow from right to left. This is a small detail but extremely important for maintaining good prosperity luck for the household.

The Rule on Water Flows is that for houses which face a secondary direction such as SW, a flow of water as in a river, canal or drain must flow from right to left. This ensures a continuity of wealth luck. For houses that face a primary direction such as North, South, East or West, the flow of water should move from left to right.

Thereafter, these flows of water can then exit the house according to the **Water Dragon Formula** on water flows. For those who are unfamiliar with this water formula, it is enough that water passing the main door flows past it correctly. Those unsure of exit directions can deal with the problem by covering their drains so that from the skies, the exit of water via drains from any property

Above: **This fall of water, which causes water in the pool to flow towards my main door is turned on four times a day, creating a flow of wealth and prosperity luck. It is important that water does not appears to flow away from the main door, as this symbolizes wealth flowing out.**

Open plan living subscribes to the view that it is not necessary to separate domestic activities into separate rooms, closed in by walls. Better to feel spacious.

Above: **I designed our drains to flow according to the Water Dragon formula. This way all water flows ourt via an auspicous exit direction . Shown here is a well where water collects before flowing out of the property. Such a small detail but an important one. A wrong exit flow can cause loss of wealth.**

is not visible. This ensures that the water is not seen to exit from an unlucky direction. For my house, being perfectly familiar with the formula, my drains flow correctly and exit correctly too.

Having attended to this matter, my preference for the practice of water feng shui is to focus on the design and location of my pools and ponds. This is because I am a business woman for whom bodies of water are more significant in terms of feng shui consideration than the flow of water…

Flow Inwards

In the pool that directly faces the main entrance, I have installed a small waterfall feature which gets activated four times a day. This creates a waterfall effect of water flowing into the pool, and then the body of water appearing to flow inwards towards the house. The flow of water towards the house as opposed to flowing away from the house is very significant. Water which appears to flow away from the house literally takes the wealth away from the home.

I personally know of several very potent examples of this having happened to some business tycoon friends of mine both here and in Hong Kong. For them, the water they installed to make their corporate head office look more attractive had their water flowing OUT and all eventually lost control of their businesses! A feng shui consultation I did in Singapore had a pool whose water overflowed away from the house. For this rich family, the outward flow was felt throughout their business. Sales declined dramatically and it was only after they built the overflow wall a little higher to reverse the direction of water that their business recovered. So those of you creating a water feature to energize the front part of your house must make sure any water flowing should be inwards and not outwards.

Looking Inwards

I ensure that the entrance area to our home is spacious, allowing the flow of energy to move easily. It is important when looking inwards into the home that there is a feeling of depth. When the view inside is "shallow", then whatever good feng shui created will not last beyond one generation. Those familiar with the houses built by immigrant Chinese traders who came to settle in Singapore, Indonesia and Malaysia

will notice that most of these homes were built long and narrow. They make up the city townhouses of successful trading families of previous generations. Many have been beautifully preserved in Singapore and anyone can come and view them to appreciate how long and deep these houses were, sometimes as many as 5 to 6 rooms deep and usually also with an open skywell to allow rain to fall directly into the home.

Our home is also long and deep. We have a depth of five rooms and our fish pond inside the house also receives fresh rain water as it is open to the skies too. I believe that this ensures there is always more than enough "heaven chi" flowing into the home to mingle auspiciously with the earth chi, thereby creating the vital trinity of *tien ti ren* – heaven, earth and mankind chi energy.

Nine Dragons
My secret friend in nine manifestations bring good fortune

A large and exceptionally powerful Nine Dragon Screen in 24 carat gold holds center stage at the foyer entrance; from the main door looking in, no one can miss the presence of the nine golden dragons hung high on the wall just below the ceiling.

The coiling dragons signify the nine sons of the dragons and their presence inside the house ALSO benefits both my husband and me. Why? Because the Dragon is the secret friend of the Rooster (me); and it is also the astrological ally of my husband, born Rat. The Dragon's presence in the home hugely benefits us both! The Dragon is also exceptionally special to Jennifer who is born in the year of the Snake as the Snake and Dragon together create the House of Magic! Hence all these years having the Dragon in the house benefited the three of us handsomely – perhaps that is why she married a Dragon! Chris her husband is a Dragon and theirs is a marriage made in heaven… their sons Jack and Josh also benefit very much from the Dragons in my home. Jack is a Monkey which makes him an ally of the Dragon! Josh is a Rat and that too makes him an ally of the Dragon. So every member of my immediate family has a connection with the mighty Dragon. Maybe that is why our family has such affinity to the living skill of feng shui, and for me personally, why the Dragon years were years of such great significance for me.

Lucky Symbols
Toads, Ammonites & Other Images

As I am a strong believer of symbolic feng shui, There is a huge variety of auspicious and lucky enhancers. Their presence in my home exudes happy vibrations. For instance there are any number of three-legged toads hidden under sofas, under tables or sitting on flower pots.

The **three-legged toad** pulls in money luck and these are very popular amongst feng shui enthusiasts of many eras. I remember when I was in Hong Kong in the Eighties ... the three legged toad was regarded as being a vital presence inside bankers' offices – indeed, it was from a banker in Hong Kong that I first came to hear about the legend of the three legged toad…

I also like **the spiral** very much as a lucky symbol; so I was not surprised when about ten years ago a feng shui master from Hong Kong, and then another one from Singapore, started promoting the ammonite as a symbol of good fortune. Actually, I was presented with a pair of very large ammonites, which must have cost quite a bomb, but shortly after displaying them inside my house, I have to confess that they did indeed bring in some amazing lucky developments, so now I too am a believer. Maybe it is because ammonites are in reality a *fossilized shells* so they are millions of years old.

In feng shui, anything that is cosmically "old" is deemed to possess greater stregnth t5han man made equivalents e.g. like the mountains and rivers – these have been affected by winds and waters over millions of years; so they possess immeasurable amounts of cosmic chi. Ammonites being spirals of millennium ages are thus considered to be concentrations of incredible power.

There are many other "lucky" symbols inside my home which get recycled and changed around frequently. I like to keep adding fresh new objects because I am sensitive to the need for constant revitalizations, so each year visitors will always feel there is something new to see. Hence I not only rearrange my furniture, I also frequently change the decorative objects, lamps, vases and porcelains put on display, especially in my living area and near the entrance sector of the house. Having said that, there are always some staples that

Top: A king frog sits in the South corner of my home.
Middle: An ammonite shell, given to me by one of my students.
Bottom: This set of ivory Ming horses was brought into our home about 30 years ago. My husband and I found them in a Singapore antique shop and fell in love with them immediately.

I feel have a permanent place in my home, and these are the celestials - the Dragons and Phoenixes, the Pi Yaos and the Gods of Wealth.

Together with the tortoises and toads, they are the perennial favourites of most people who believe in feng shui. So for these items, I might replace the old one with newer better looking models, but they have a permanent place in my home...

Animal Allies

In addition to auspicious objects, I also subscribe to the power of astrological influences on the feng shui of my house. Ever since I discovered the amazing benefits of activating one's astrological allies and secret friends in our home, I have pursued this dimension of feng shui with single-minded focus.

So you can imagine my huge jubilation when I found that a supplier had brought a jade Ox to me which connected instantly with my psyche. This Ox has a small gem quality pocket of jade that is so green it looks like my jade ring, and this rests lightly on the shoulder of the Ox. Naturally I kept the Ox and invited it home where it resides happily under one of my altar tables with other auspicious creatures.

For those unfamiliar with the 12 astrology signs of the Chinese Zodiac, let me explain that the Ox is my ally, because the Ox and the Rooster are allies. But I am married to a Rat, and the Ox and Rat are secret friends; hence having a jade Ox inside my home displayed near the entrance brings excellent relationship and other kinds of luck for the both of us. In fact, the Ox is the animal sign that brings the Rat and Rooster closer to each other. Indeed, of all our mutual friends, it is always those born in the Year of the Ox who are the closest to the both of us!

And so because the Ox is so vital to us both, I have also placed beautifully carved images of the Ox in its form as the bull in other parts of my home.

My home also has many varieties of **Roosters** which I place in the West (the direction of the Rooster) and also a great many **Rat** images which I place around the pond in the North sector of the home. My Rats are usually bejeweled and come sitting on a bed of ingots – basically this is to symbolically benefit my husband! The presence of one's animal sign (or Earthly

Above: I love this Jade Rooster which my dear friend and business associate Peter Lung hand carried to Malaysia all the way from the USA to present to me as his family's gift to me for my 60th birthday. It is an exceptionally beautiful piece and I treasure it for all the sentiments that came with it. Peter and Joanie Lung live with their two lovely daughters Lauren and Ashley in Las Vegas and it was feng shui that caused my family and theirs to become firm friends. I use this Jade Rooster to energize my golden nine dragon screen!

Above: This is the crystal bull which my staff at the Hong Kong based Dao Heng Bank presented to me as a farewell gift when I left the Bank in the mid-Eighties. It is made of crystal and inside are 24 carat gold specks, something I consider most auspicious - so I have had this bull for over twenty years now... and I do like to think that it has brought me great prosperity luck over the years.

Branch) in the home, especially when they look "rich and abundant" is extremely beneficial. It is also excellent to display the animal sign of the year when its year comes around, especially when the animal is also your astrological ally, your secret friend or has a seasonal affinity with you. All the significant astrological associations between the Zodiac animal signs are fully explained in the annual **Fortune & Feng Shui** books on the animal signs which Jennifer and I publish each year.

Pair of Pi Zie
containing ingots to accumulate wealth

I am very fond of this pair of antique Pi Zies which I was lucky enough to pick up several years ago. They are quite old and their design indicates having been made around the turn of the last century, although they do not come with "papers".

Usually I do not like bringing "old" stuff into my home as I am always wary of the energy that sticks to old furniture and decorative objects, but there was something about this pair that grabbed me. They are incense burners and since I am a firm believer in the incense ritual for dissolving obtacles I liked their energy. However I do not use them as incense burners.

When inviting antique pieces into the home, it is a good idea to symbolically cleanse them with natural rock salt to ensure you remove any negative energy that may be lingering.

Instead, I filled them to contain faux gold ingots in a ritualistic enhancement of prosperity luck. Somehow I felt that these Pi Zies exuded the energy of wealth luck – so I went with my instincts.

Whether or not they have brought extra wealth luck does not matter as much as how much joy they give me just looking at them.

Before filling them with real money and ingots however, I used a mixture of sea and rock salt to symbolically cleanse the pair of whatever bad lingering energy they may be having. All you need to do is use the salt to wipe with downward strokes several times and then use a damp cloth soaked also in salt to wipe it through. This is one of the easier ways of getting rid of whatever bad energy may be clinging to antique pieces. It is important to do this ritual as soon as you bring them into the home. Remember to use natural rock salt.

Top: The female of the pair of antique Pi Zie which I invited into my home eight years ago. I bought them from a shop which brings in some exceptional items but they were unable to tell me the provenance of this pair. I liked them so much, i got them anyway.

Next page: You can see that this pair of Pi Zie were once used as incense burners. I love their fierce countenance so I use them as as symbolic protecters of the family's asset wealth. I keep them half filled with faux gold ingots. This leaves room for more to enter.

PART 2
MY LIVING AREA

It is obvious to anyone visiting my house for the first time to feel instantly how airy the home is, and also how open the living halls are. Light pours into the home from all directions and most mornings the sun is so bright it is almost blinding. This is because the doors are kept open through the day.

The next thing thnat strikes the visitor are my Buddhas. They are everywhere, in every room, large and small, sitting and standing, colourful or gold leafed, and all having different mudras - ie hand gestures that have different meanings. My thangkas and my statues do reveal my great passion for holy objects especially Buddha images that are works of art, sculpted as well as painted. I also have stupas, prayer wheels and what I call tsa tsas - miniature plaster Buddha images that we make ourselves using special rubber moulds purchased from nalanda Monastery. These sit majestically in rows on the walls of my home.

MAIN HALL
comprising three main rooms in an open space concept

Above: **The large TV screen in this part of the home was placed here for feng shui reasons. The television is kept turned on from early evening to the nocturnal hours. This generates noise and activity causing the energy to move and flow. When there is no one around we keep the noise level down, but we always make sure that the heart of the home is never kept silent for too long.**

Right: **A beautiful quartz crystal decorated with powerful mantras, written onto the crystal with gold pen by Charok Lama Rinpoche.**

We spend plenty of time in the main part of the home. This is our living area and it basically comprises "three rooms", two of which were part of the original house, but now with an old wall and a large door to ceiling entrance removed.

The "foyer" part of the living area connects the East side with the West side of the home and this used to be the outside patio of the original house. We brought this part of the house inside together with the fish pond and it has now become a focal area where a special altar has been placed.

There is a small foyer which serves to welcome in the energy from the Southeast door. Here a long sideboard serves as the display area for some important feng shui display items:

- the Wealth God bringing in gold carried on a tribute horse

- the Ox bringing gold ingots to signify luck being brought in this year

- the Green Cabbage Fatt Choy signifying a hundred kinds of good fortune

- Crystal Apples for peace and harmony

- carved images of Kuan Yin in various kinds of crystal gemstones

The original garage is now the East wing and this is being used as my Buddhist gompa, or puja hall. This is where I hold my monthly prayer sessions with my Buddhist friends; and when it is not being used as a gompa, my second grandchild romps on the thickly carpeted floor. It is a very nice part of the home and we do spend quite a bit of time here.

The main part of the living area was my original living room and although it is small by today's standards, we thought it was quite a respectable size back then in the 1970s. This is where I chat with really good friends and where we sing and watch television together. Actually, it is also the "center" of the house, so it qualifies to be described as the heart of the home. You can say that the essence of the home is right here. It is very

auspicious that the yang energy created here continues to beat vigorously. I placed a very big television screen in this center part of the house to ensure that each time we sit down to watch some high definition television with friends or by ourselves, the heart of the home automatically gets activated with sounds and motion. The images of the television create excellent feng shui and because I really only watch happy movies, popular concerts and musicals, what gets shown is always happy stuff.

This not only ensures the creation of happiness vibrations, it also ensures the good health of my family members. The strong chi that is produced here daily also keeps us all very vibrant with life and this in turn ensures that the chi strength of the home stays strong. Feng shui is about energy and good feng shui requires one to constantly keep the chi moving, flowing and active. Good feng

shui requires not just updating, but it also needs to be maintained. Unless you make the effort to prevent chi stagnation, the energy of any house is sure to get tired and go to sleep. And that is when illness and bad luck starts to happen.

Heart of the Home

I make sure the heart of the home pulsates with active energy, so here is where I sit down with my neverending stream of visitors. I have many different groups of friends so there is never a problem filling the home with laughter and the sounds of friendship. I do not think of this as entertaining and indeed, I almost never give formal dinner parties. But there is always food in the refrigerator to welcome drop-in visitors.

Above: **I regularly invite my close Dharma friends over for pujas. Pictured above is my prayer hall where I maintain our main altar. This used to be the garage in the Seventies and the house used to face this direction of Southeast. This part of the home looks out to the left dragon side so I have kept the windows low here; to welcome in the Dragon energy from this left side of the house. This picture was taken during a special puja session held during Moon Festival this year.**

Children exude the purest form of yang chi so having my two grandsons here replenishes the pure yang chi of the house like nothing else can!

Everyone who visits appreciates the relaxed and casual ambience of my home and I make sure they feel welcome and relaxed. You do not need to dress up to come visit. Nor do you need to stand on ceremony. I am home most of the time because I do love spending time at home.

I also work from here, and indeed have two offices where I check my emails, surf the internet and write my books, so I am usually at home when people drop by... and then they will eat what I eat and sort of just roll into my day...

Most of the time the daylight hours are when my grandsons come and spend time with me. Jack comes everyday; and he does a variety of things with me... including watching high definition television. His favourite is **Casino Royale**, the James Bond movie starring **Daniel Craig** and we have watched it together now over thirty times. He is fascinated by the poker games and

has since mastered poker to an extent that surprises us all. We figure using poker to teach him mental arithmetic and the concept of probabilities is not a bad idea at all...

Jack has also become quite the expert on mahjong which he plays with me and his grandfather. We indulge him because card games and mahjong are such a fun way of teaching him numbers and game strategy... he is five years old and has started school and of course his spending time with us means so much to us. Josh is four years younger than Jack and being born in the Rat Year makes him an ally of Jack, so they get along very well. He too spends plenty of time in my house.

Children exude the purest form of yang chi, so having my two grandsons here, especially when they have their afternoon nap in the heart of my home, well, this replenishes the pure yang chi of the house like nothing else can! And because they are usually very relaxed and happy while here, this gives me the reassurance that the feng shui energy is fine. If it were not, they would be fretful and weepy. Children are more sensitive to the quality of energy than adults.

Generating Yang Chi

Feng shui differentiates between houses of the living and houses of the dead, and while BOTH kinds of houses create powerful impact on the quality of a family's feng shui, it is the houses of the living that are of greater importance. In fact I leave cemeteries and burial grounds pretty much alone. In any case, I prefer cremating, so *yin feng shui* holds little interest for me.

In houses of the living, YANG energy is very important. If you want to enjoy vibrant good feng shui, then you must design your living space and establish living habits that create copious supplies of yang chi.

This means having lots of **bright lights, sounds** and **motion** in your living space. Keep your spaces well lit; make sure there are no stagnant dark corners where yin energy might possibly accumulate. When it does, yin can bring stagnation to your luck. And always have some kind of movement, something going on, some life energy... in the house.

For light, sunshine is the best source during the day time hours, so windows or sky lights that allow the sun to come in are important. One of the best ways of bringing the sunshine indoors is by hanging **reflective crystal balls** along windows that catch the direct sun. These create rainbows inside the home, and these bring powerful chi energy inwards. If sunlight is not available, then use artificial warm light to infuse your spaces with light ambience. To create good feng shui, warm yellow light is always to be preferred to white cool light.

All round the living areas of the home there should be **a variety of living sounds**. Think of breezes blowing, of water flowing, or metals clinking, or music playing, people talking, and anything else that suggests

Above: I hang facetted crystal balls from the branch of the Bodhi tree in my garden. These drops of crystal capture the sunlight each morning and evening giving off the most brilliant sparks of rainbow, making the garden come alive with quite magical chi energy.

Above: **My stunning Bodhi tree drips with exquisite facetted crystals. The Bodhi tree is regarded with reverence by Buddhists as Shakyamuni Buddha attained enlightenment meditating under a Bodhi tree.**

activity and life. Hence dogs barking, birds chirping, the radio turned on, babies gurgling and little children laughing are good examples of auspicious home sounds that are sure to up the quality of yang chi in your environment.

> When your home is alive with the constant occurrence of these sounds of living, then vibrant yang chi is present.

These sounds are especially important if yours is a two-person household and you both work, so the house is left empty and quiet the whole day. For you, keeping a pet at home to create life chi is one solution. Another is to keep the radio or TV turned on through the day, even if you are both out.

There should also be **movement** in the living space...so I keep fans turned on and this creates gentle breezes inside the home. Besides, there are always people dropping by visiting me, so they bring activity and movement too.

Also, because mine is a very big house, we share the house with **four beautiful dogs**, two of whom, my beautiful golden Cocker Spaniels, **Juno** and **Chester**, live indoors and two, my stunning American Golden Retrievers, **Jumbo** and **Google**, live outdoors.

> I have kept dogs all my life. I do not recall there ever being a time in my life when I did not have a dog as a pet, so they are loved and cosseted as part of my family. They bring excellent feng shui because I know my love for them is matched only by their love for me... so they create plenty of loving chi.

I also share my home with dozens of **birds** – magpies who nest in the eaves of my roofs, and tons of **squirrels** who feed on my fruit trees. Then of course there are my fish – gold fish, carp and feng shui fish. I love feeding them every morning and their living here with me signifies an abundance of abundance – for this is exactly what fish means in feng shui. I have a big house, so I feel it is really good to share my home with these fellow creatures of this planet. So yes, there are plentiful amounts of living chi in my home!

Above: **Himalayan incense sticks and pine leaves make up the ingredients for smoke offerings performed to appease the local "landlords" every Friday. I use burning charcoal to bring out the aromas of the pine leaves.**

Facing page: **My husband Wan Jin and I enjoying what has become quite a paradise of a garden. I like to feel that our home helps us to grow old gracefully...**

To ensure that the house energy stays active and alive all the time, I make sure there is absolutely no clutter, so all paraphernalia of daily living is kept neatly stored inside cupboards, which are cleared out every month. I am most particular about this. Old newspapers and wrappings are sold as scrap every week and magazines are nicely stacked in coffee table shelves.

There are plenty of auspicious objects that reflect the five elements of feng shui, discreetly placed all over the house. Healthy plants placed inside the house are rotated every month so plants look healthy.

And of course, there are wealth pots, wealth vases, a whole harbour of sailing ships, plenty of embroidered mystical knots and other lucky symbols hanging on walls, placed on display tables and fresh scents that keep the house smelling good always; candles in the evening are offerings to my Buddhas, but they also add a beautiful understated ambience.

Meanwhile, singing bowl rituals created daily lift the chi, while incense and smoke offerings to the local "landlords" are performed every Friday.

Then there are the crystal singing bowls which generate the most amazing vibration-type music... and this is usually done before my morning chat with my goldfish, my dogs and my plants. I believe that everything – living and dead – exudes some kind of energy, so I embrace them all into my mandala.

There is always music playing discreetly in the background and since my husband and I like many kinds of music, our repertoire includes almost every kind of music – from popular to classical... golden oldies to popular music... and plenty of beautiful sacred music including mantras recited by some of the most beautiful voices in the world.

Focus Northwest

One theory of feng shui has it that the corner that is diagonally opposite the entrance main door is the "power spot" of the home. This means that this part of the home is potentially very auspicious, and paying attention to the feng shui of this corner brings long-lasting benefits.

Above: **The Northwest of our house is diagonal from my husband's SE main door. I ensure that this part of the house is well activated at all times with lucky objects, as this corner signifies the luck of the Patriarch.**

Always protect the NW and SW sectors of the home, as these signify the luck of the Father and the Mother.

For us, this corner corresponds exactly to the Northwest sector of the house. It is also diagonally opposite the door that faces Southeast which is our "patriarchal door" so to speak. And the Northwest is also the Patriarchal sector, so here is where my husband's luck resides!

To maintain good luck for my husband, I keep a light here perpetually turned on, and although the element of the Northwest is Metal, and the presence of Fire energy brings fire to heaven's gate, the light I have here signifies yin fire. There are no open fires here, but the presence of a bright light here ensures the presence of the all important yang chi. Note that the Northwest also stands for **mentor luck** so I know that it is really important to hang a painting of the Buddha in this corner. In my mind, there is no mentor more meaningful or more powerful than the **Buddha Shakyamuni** himself.

There used to be a small store room placed here originally in the Northwest when the house was first built. I did not realize at that time that this would have a very negative and restrictive effect on my husband's feng shui, as it symbolically "locked" up his career luck. We completely overlooked this all-important matter at that time.

That was also when our knowledge of feng shui was quite amateurish and it was not until many years later that I noticed it, and immediately then had the store room removed. I did this by opening up the area. Instantly my husband's luck improved, actually quite substantially. These days I make certain the Northwest is kept activated at all times with lucky objects. I also placed a refrigerator here to symbolize a store of food. This signifies abundance and good fortune for the patriarch, so no wonder my husband has lots to eat, and in his retirement is definitely enjoying life. As a reminder to readers, do note that it is so important that store rooms, toilets and kitchens should never be located in either the Southwest or the Northwest – these two locations represent the well being and energy of the mother and father of the house. Hurting these two prime members of any household is bound to harm the whole family. For exactly the same reason, neither of these corners should be missing.

When the Northwest sector of any home is missing, it creates the bad luck feng shui of a missing patriarch. This can mean that unmarried women in the household will find it difficult to get married.

Their husband luck will be missing; or it can also mean that the husband of the house is frequently away from home, either travelling a great deal or even having an alternative family outside (i.e. with a second wife). The same effect will be experienced when the SW corner is missing, except instead of the father, it refers to the mother.

In my house, I make absolutely certain that both corners are not only not missing, but that they are also well energized, kept free of clutter and the energy is not left to stagnate in any way.

One of the basic feng shui methods in which I have a great deal of faith is the *Eight Sector Eight Aspirations* method which is easy to understand and just as easy to use. This method is also a quick way of harnessing the different kinds of energies intrinsically present in each of the sectors of the home. The eight sectors of the home signify eight types of luck which are termed aspirations.

According to this method of feng shui, if you have these eight types of luck – a good name, a regular source of income, increasing asset wealth, good marriage and family luck, good descendants luck, good health luck and longevity, meaningful wisdom and the support of influential/powerful friends – then you are deemed to be enjoying excellent feng shui. Every household should thus endeavour to enjoy these eight kinds of good fortune.

What the method entails is simply to demarcate your home into eight different compass sectors and within each sector to arrange the space, display a suitable lucky item and then energize the sector according to the sector's element to attract one of the eight kinds of luck.

What this means for me is that I make sure that I "energize" each of the sectors with the right kind of auspicious decorative item. I can also use the five element method of activating the energy of each sector, and this means adding to the store of water, wood, fire, earth or metal chi in particular sectors. For me, this is a very easy way of making sure I enjoy good feng shui throughout the year.

I have to explain that I have been using this easy way of enhancing my feng shui for a very long time, in fact, ever since I started believing in feng shui. At first I would use simple things like candles and plants, decorative stones, round and square boxes, coins and red paper… but as I got more sophisticated in my wants and desires, I noticed that I began using increasingly more expensive and better made decorative objects. These actually brought greater success and I have been upgrading ever since!

My South Sector

This is a very important corner for me as the quality of the energy here directly influences my good name and has a bearing on the continued success and popularity of my books. As such, I go to great lengths to ensure there is always vibrant fire element chi here. This is the element of the South and having yang lights here (preferably moving) is exactly right for this sector.

I keep a very bright light here always turned on and the latest activator here is a fabulous ingot light which moves around in a clockwise direction continuously creating yang chi…

On the floor and on the display table is my collection of ivory Ming-style horses in various poses. Horses are incredible symbols of speed, endurance and success to have in the home. The horse is also my peach blossom animal, so for me personally, the presence of horses in the South not only energizes the sector, they also bring me plenty of love luck!

Meanwhile, perched on the two half moon tables here is a wooden carving of the Goddess Kuan Yin sitting on a Phoenix. This is very meaningful because the phoenix is also associated with the South. But more than that, phoenixes are said to be the heavenly manifestation of the earthly

The Eight Aspirations method is a quick way of harnessing the different kinds of energies intrinsically present in each of the sectors of the home.

Above: **Kuan Yin sitting on a Phoenix takes pride of place in the South corner of my living area.**

Rooster. So for us, the phoenix bringing the Goddess Kuan Yin into my home is very auspicious.

The horses here also activate the sector's importance as my peach blossom direction. Their presence creates good vibrations for my marriage and my family luck. Family harmony is vital for there to be peace and happiness in the home.

Because the South is also my husband's *nien yen* direction, the feng shui enhancers that I have placed here directly benefits him as well. This is his Kua formula direction that improves and maintains his family luck! So for my family, the South sector is an important part of the house. If it had been missing, then my marriage luck would have suffered. In the period of 6 when the house was first built, the garage occupied what is now the South sector, so it was not so auspicious then.

My Southeast & East Sectors

Another corner that I deem extremely important is the Southeast wall of my East living room.

The Southeast is the sector that governs **wealth luck**, the kind of wealth associated with asset accumulation and increasing of the family's net worth with each passing year.

This is a very important dimension of good feng shui, and the Masters who practise it in Hong Kong and Taiwan are very particular about paying attention to this part of homes, simply because the safeguarding of family wealth is such an intrinsic dimension of good feng shui.

My Southeast sector is actually my boundary wall outside where I have "grown" a Dragon ever since living here. This means I have planted different kinds of plants to simulate the presence of the Dragon. Each year, the Taoist Master comes to "activate the spirit of the Dragon" by reciting special incantations in this part of the house.

This is wonderful Taoist feng shui and it ensures that as a family we will continue to enjoy good wealth luck. With the presence of the Dragon – as evidenced by plenty of lush

growing plants, there is no necessity then to place water here.

But each year I do take advantage of the Taoist master's presence to enquire about the well-being and health of my resident "Dragon". This is important to us continuing to enjoy good feng shui as a "vibrant healthy Dragon" is crucial to any house maintaining its good fortune flows of energy. Usually, when your Dragon spirit is weak, then the Taoist Master can recite some incantations that will strengthen it. Thankfully, my Dragon spirit continues to be in good health and good spirits.

Meanwhile, inside the house I have also placed various kinds of Dragons lining the Southeast wall, as this brings the energy of the Dragons indoors. Since my whole family has so much affinity with the Dragon, exaggerating its presence in the home can only bring benefits!

Just consider…

My husband, the Rat-born is an *ally* of the Dragon. Me, a Rooster is the *secret friend* of the Dragon. Jennifer, a Snake creates the *House of Magic* with the Dragon. Chris, our son-in-law is himself a Dragon born! Jack (a Monkey) and Josh (a Rat) - my two grandsons - are *allies* of the Dragon.

From a feng shui perspective, every member of my direct family benefits from activating the Dragon in the Southeast/East wing of my house. Maybe everyone feels so embraced in my home because the spirit of the Dragon is so strong here that as a family we have all benefited greatly from the Dragon magic of our living space.

Golden Dragons
Secret Friend activated

Most significantly is the presence of the nine golden dragons placed high above the Southwest-facing wall looking out to draw the good energy into the house. This is meant to benefit me directly, so a most precious jade Rooster (given to me by my good friend Peter Lung) looks directly at the Dragons. This is very important to get

Facing Page: **What could be more auspicious than two Dragons frolicking atop an ingot?**

Above: **A yellow porcelain vase with a Dragon, another one of my collection of Dragons, this one from my days in Hong Kong**.

Right: This is an incense holder that is perfect for the INCENSE pujas I hold regularly to generate harmony chi with no obstacles..

maximum benefits from the presence of the Dragons.

Those of you wanting to reap the kind of benefits I have been reaping from the Dragon, you can only do what I do if your animal sign of birth has an affinity with the Dragon. Thus those of you born in the year of the Rooster can activate the secret friendship with the Dragon, while Rats and Monkeys can energize their ally association with the Dragon. The Snake and the Dragon also have affinity as they are Zodiac soul mates who create magic together.

Those of you born in the year of the Dog however should be wary of the Dragon! For you, and also for those born in the years of the Sheep, it is better to activate the presence of the fearless Horse in the South, your ally and secret friend respectively. The Horse is also regarded as an auspicious animal to invite into the home.

In my home there are plenty of Dragons because our **affinity is with the Dragon**, and I place them everywhere. So in addition to my golden Dragons, I also have crystal Dragons, porcelain Dragons, enameled Dragons embellished with crystals as well as Dragons made of fabulous Liu Li.

These celestial creatures have really brought big benefits into my life and there is simply no denying their significance to my luck. So there will always be room for these celestial creatures... as you saw earlier when I shared significant Dragon years with you, and the way it always surfaces in my life just when I least expect it to - and then always bringing some kind of good thing to me...

Another excellent creature to activate maximum luck is the fast, brave and courageous Horse. This animal is the secret friend of the Sheep, the ally of the Dog and Tiger, and the Peach Blossom animal of the Ox, Rooster and Snake. Hence any of these animal signs can place images of the Horse in their home. For this reason, I also have a big collection of horses, which I place mainly in the South.

Flashback to HBS

I spent two years 1974 to 1976 in Boston USA attending the Harvard B School - the B here stands for Business. I was a graduate student of HBS; working towards the two year MBA degree. I had been inspired to apply while working at the Malaysian Industrial Development Authority (MIDA).

My job at MIDA entailed meeting foreign investors keen on setting up manufacturing operations here. Malaysia in those years had a strategy to attract big name electronic manufacturers from the United States and there were quite a number who did come – companies such as Intel, Motorola, National Semiconductor… whose executives came to meet with us to set up operations here. Many were either lawyers or MBA types and I was very impressed by them. I liked their easy confidence, and was excited by what they told me about American graduate schools, especially their business schools.

Getting accepted into Harvard was a stroke of pure luck. I had been warned that getting in could be tough. But I think I wrote a good application and I got high scores in the GMAT. I also used a little known Taoist method of energizing my application with success energy - by placing a red dot on the envelope that contained my application.

Harvard was a happy time – those years opened my eyes wide to everything the world had to offer and although I was barely able to keep up with the hot shot clever American kids, I'm glad to say that in the end I did graduate rather well. Business school taught me basic skills in finance and management but I think more importantly, it built my confidence, and gave me an air of knowing that would serve me incredibly well for the rest of my life!

Left: **At Harvard B School. Business School taught me basic skills in finance & management but more importantly it built my confidence and gave me an air of knowing that would serve me well all my life. Here I am silhouetted against Baker Library at HBS.**

Above: **On an auspicious day - the anniversary of Buddha's descent to Earth - I arranged for the mantras on the giant wheel to be covered in real 24K gold leaf.**

Rolled into this gigantic prayer wheel are over 68 billion mantras of "Omani Padme Hum". So each spin of the wheel activates the mantra 68 billion times!

Facing Page: **The magnificent wheel when it first got completed. Today it is a different colour, after the copper got painted and the mantras and symbols got gold leafed.**

Prayer Wheel
in my West Sector

The Eight Aspirations method describes the West part of the home as the place where a family's **descendents luck** can be activated. If you place a **pink lotus** in the West for instance, it helps childless couples conceive!

For me, the West has the added significance of it being the astrological location of the **Rooster**, my animal sign. So keeping this part of the house vibrant and strong benefits me personally as well.

Here the element is Metal and it is also the part of the house best suited to the ageing matriarchs of the family. So this is also where I have a suite of rooms specially designed for **my ageing mother** who is now 85 years old. She suffers from dementia and Alzheimer's disease and I have a full-time maid looking after her… she has been living with me ever since my Dad passed away fifteen years ago. I like to think she is reasonably happy living here even though she no longer recognizes any of us. But she smiles a lot and there is a restful relaxed look to her countenance. Her health is also excellent and she eats and sleeps well, so I believe she is reasonably comfortable.

But for some time I felt that surely there must be something more I can do to benefit her. The solution sort of came on its own… probably a reflection of her good karma and mine, I guess, because late in 2008, I actually succeeded in building a giant size **Golden Prayer Wheel** here that not only strengthened the metal element of the West, but also brought immense spiritual benefits for my mother and our whole family.

I consider this something of a miracle really because as those of you who have firsthand experience of caring for someone with Alzheimer's, you will know that they in effect have completely lost their minds… and it is the saddest thing in the world to watch them, especially when you remember how alive and vibrant they used to be. For me, watching my mother when she has that lost look in her eyes really tugs at me and I have to swallow very hard not to give way to my tears… it would only confuse her.

But now in turning the prayer wheel daily, she accumulates amazing karmic merit and without having to even know what she is doing, she is gaining merit! This is because there are billions of mantras rolled inside this magnificent prayer wheel. Turning it as she does daily is like reciting the powerful mantras contained inside! Honestly, I cannot imagine anything more beneficial than this amazing prayer wheel! That she now smiles a whole lot more tells me that in some innermost recesses of her mind, somehow she knows it too and it is making her happy.

68 Billion Mantras!

More than feng shui, I believe in the amazing power of mantras… and the presence of an amazing **Golden Prayer Wheel** in my home somehow is a manifestation of the great power of mantras. Rolled into this gigantic wheel which spins smoothly on its German-made ball bearings, are over 68 billion mantras of *Omani Padme Hum*, the six syllable mantra of the Compassionate Buddha. Each spin of the wheel activates this mantra 68 billion times, so the energy of the mantras reverberates outwards in increasingly expanding concentric rings of blessings. My mind boggles at the thought! The thought of its ever expanding circles of blessings is awesome indeed.

This is the largest prayer wheel in Malaysia and Singapore. Its existence was inspired by the beautiful large prayer wheels I saw around the **Boudhanath** and **Swayambunath** stupas in Katmandu and at Kopan Monastery.

Every year that I was there I saw such devotion on the faces of all those who came just to turn the prayer wheels that the seed of the idea of building a similar wheel in my home must surely have taken root then.

But I think I was inspired most of all by **Lama Zopa Rinpoche**, who has been the direct cause of building so many beautiful Prayer wheels around the world. When he suggested I might like to build a prayer wheel in my house in 2007 I jumped at the idea. If Rinpoche suggests it, I know that it means I must have the karma to do it!

We were together in Lawado at that time, in the Solu Khumbu region of the Himalayas. That was when we had hiked up the Himalayas together, an amazing journey that had literally taken my breath away.

Rinpoche's suggestion resonated so strongly with me that I lost no time in getting the whole project organized as soon as I got home, and the speed with which it all came to be amazed me as much as it did Rinpoche, who flew to Malaysia specially to consecrate it some months later.

Above: **Lama Zopa Rinpoche doing a special puja to consecrate the new prayer wheel. Pictured in the foreground above also are smaller prayer wheels which were given to those who wished to "sponsor" them to help Rinpoche's monastery in Katmandu. Each of these small prayer wheels contain over 100 million mantras.**

The prayer wheel was finished in Nov 2008 and was consecrated in Feb 2009. In all it took 4 months; it is made by skilled craftsmen in Katmandu, then dismantled and air flown to Kuala Lumpur where the craftsmen came to install it in my home.

Meanwhile, I had arranged for the mantras to be printed in microfilm to boost the number of mantras that I can roll into the wheel into the billions. Inside the wheel however are more than the *Omani padme hum* mantras. We also included ten million of the ten most powerful mantras and also the complete Kangyur and eight sets of the **Zung Du.** These are amazing Buddhist texts that are precious and powerful and their presence here in my home ensures there is always a radiating charisma of divine blessings.

It is no small thing having a personal prayer wheel so large and containing so many holy texts. What it means is that it is really easy for me to practise. All I need to do really to accumulate good karmic merit is simply to turn the wheel each morning and each evening! Surely this has to be the best feng shui possible!

Mountain at the Back Water in Front

We are very lucky because the natural inclination of our property makes it easy to follow the most important of feng shui guidelines which is to have Mountain at the back and Water in front. Our back is also Northeast which stands for the mountain, and it is also the direction of the current period. This makes the sitting palace of our home - the *direct spirit* of this Period 8 - auspicious and with the presence of higher land behind, this naturally creates the mountain.

When the direct spirit is activated by the presence of higher land or the mountain, it brings auspicious networking and mentor luck. All relationships forged with outsiders bring luck to the family.

So the higher land at the back makes our environmental feng shui excellent.

The property behind us is owned by a very wealthy family and this makes it doubly auspicious as it means we are symbolically supported by a rich mountain. Also, our facing direction of Southwest 1 places the mountain star 8 at the back of this house, so it is being activated by the higher land. As a result, the health and relationship aspect of our luck is at a very good level.

Meanwhile, the front Southwest is the direction of the *indirect spirit* of the current period of 8. Having water at the front automatically activates the indirect spirit generating prosperity luck. More, our water star 8 is at the front based on the flying star chart. And *sarn he* feng shui criteria of having water in front is also met. Hence the presence of water at our front brings excellent wealth luck for the family.

Our house thus meets both the *landscape* criteria of good feng shui as well as the *compass* formula criteria. This is generally what most feng shui practitioners strive to achieve.

It is not always easy to achieve and usually there is a big element of luck. Indeed, when we first bought our land here, it was really the best we could afford at that time and we chose it simply on the basis of our gut feel. At that time, both my husband and I were rather vague in our knowledge of feng shui... so we were lucky!

Above: We spent nearly a week gilding the wheel with real gold. It was a long process but can you imagine the merit of offering gold to 68 billion mantras! Pictured here with my dear friends Cindy and Juanita who helped me with this task.
Below: Rolling the mantras inside the prayer wheel. There are 68 billion in all!

Depth & Breadth
& Wonderful Moonlight

The house as it stands today has depth – being five rooms deep – and this is good feng shui. This ensures that our good fortune luck has the potential to last five generations. But of course it was not always so good. When the house was first built, it was only three rooms deep, which is not bad but not great either.

Today, the house definitely has a good feeling of endurance... and I feel confident that there is continuity of luck in my family and this is far more important as long term luck always beats short term. When you get to be my age, the luck of your children and grandchildren also become extremely important.

What is exciting however is that we also have breadth, and while this is not as vital as having depth, nevertheless when the house is wide and spacious it creates a capacity for abundance; this is brought about by the extra garden space in the Northwest.

We removed the wall here to add a very wide patio space to this right side of the house. Here is where we enjoy outdoor living which is just excellent for the grandchildren. Plus of course a view of healthy green grass is incredibly soothing for the eye at all times. In fact, I view my garden space as our sanctuary. Not only is it visible from many angles inside the house but it is just the right size, small enough to be intimate, yet large enough for us to have a good game of anything.

As you will see later when I bring you into my garden, the plants and trees and shrubs here really feeds my soul just watching how well they grow in response to our care. Time spent in my garden is strengthening luck for me because the *self element* in my paht chee chart is weak Wood.

So the more I surround myself with wood energy, the stronger I will be. In feng shui terms, it is only when one's self element is strong that one is able to take advantage of good luck that comes one's way. The garden is of course mainly Wood element.

On nights when the whole garden gets lit up by moonlight, that is when even particles of dust turn into specks of glistening jewels...

At nights, the skies above are almost always clear so we see the moon in all its glory, from new moon and all through the fifteen days of the waxing moon. But especially during full moon nights this is when the whole garden gets lit up by the brightness of the moonlight. That is when it turns even particles of dust into glittering jewels. There is something very magical about moonlight and I am always aware of **full moon nights.** That is when I bring out many of my personal feng shui items – especially my brass mirrors and my wealth wallets to be energized by moon essence.

I also love celebrating **Mid Autumn Festival** for that is when the full moon shines the brightest of all. This is an evening to invite close friends over, have a feast of yummy dishes, eat delicious moon cakes, hang colourful lanterns and make an array of light and flower offerings to the Buddhas.

Mid Autumn can be as auspicious as the fifteenth day of the lunar new year. In fact, these are the two nights of the year when I make it a point to be at home and not travelling.

For on these nights is when I like all the doors of my house to be thrown wide open and all the lights to be turned on. These are nights when the *yang energy* of the moon is at its most powerful and its most auspicious, so letting its essence flow gently into the house revitalizes it beautifully.

Above: **My second grandson Joshy celebrates his first Moon Festival.**

Facing page: After the gold-leafing, **the prayer wheel now glistens with real gold, pictured here at night.**

Overleaf: **The house is just as beautiful at night as it is in the daytime, sometimes even more beautiful!**

Power Ru Yi

Propped prominently on my coffee table in the middle of my home is my power symbol, my very large and very solid looking Ru Yi – the ancient symbol of authority which is as relevant and meaningful today as it ever was hundreds of years ago. I have repeatedly urged many of my friends who are holding important positions in business or politics to invest in a good Ru Yi and then to place it either in their home or office.

I urged them to make the Ru Yi look prominent in their space, so that the chi energy it gives out can be both impressive and yes, slightly intimidating. It will add much to their sense of empowerment, and more importantly, add great depth to their aura of authority.

Above: **My giant Ru Yi made out of rosewood and intricately carved feature the 18 Arhats, special Holy Men from China with special powers.**

No CEO or big time politician can afford NOT to have a Ru Yi in his/her official space, as there is also an element of protection about the Ru Yi. Its presence near where you work, or in your living space, will safeguard your position and help watch that no one can successfully undermine you.

My personal Ru Yi is carved out of rosewood and several years after it came into my possession I also had it gold leafed. By now you must know that I am extremely fond of gold leafing my precious possessions, especially those that have either a spiritual meaning or a feng shui function.

The Ru Yi I have is decorated with many different auspicious symbols and celestial guardians placed as accessories to the 18 Arhats that have been skillfully carved into the Ru Yi. These special holy men of China have special powers. Their presence in any home is believed to bless the home with good fortune.

I actually have three sets of the 18 Arhats, but the 18 perched on my Ru Yi are seated on Dragon, Sheep, Pi Yao, Chi Lin, Fu Dog, Tiger, Elephant and so forth – so these celestial and special creatures are also in my Ru Yi. In addition, there are longevity pine trees, ingots, coins and wealth trees as well as peaches, cranes and bats – so my Ru Yi has them all.

As you can see from the picture, mine is a very large Ru Yi. And in case you are wondering, yes, SIZE does matter! In feng shui, when you display an important symbol of power, wealth or longevity – three important aspirations – the bigger the symbol the better! It is like the office desk, or the bed you sleep on - the bigger the better!

The Ru Yi's presence on my center coffee table definitely empowers me, endowing me with personal vigour and strength, and I believe brings me a great deal of powerful and influential friends. With this one Ru Yi, I do not need the other symbols of authority. The great thing about rosewood is that it is hard, and it is also very lucky. The longer the Ru Yi stays in my possession, the greater its ability to attract authoritative empowerments into the home. And I hope it becomes a powerful heirloom that continues to bring good fortune to Jennifer in future years.

Crystal Globes
for smooth sailing

On my coffee table in my main living room are six crystal globes – round balls made of solid crystal. I also have them in coloured glass. These are Earth element symbols that signify the power of heaven, and their inherent power to bring harmony to their environment is truly amazing.

So I advocate their presence in any home to ensure that all the projects of residents meet with success easily and effortlessly.

Below: Smooth crystal balls sit atop my main coffee table in my home. They bring harmony to the household, ensuring all family members are supportive of one another. They also make all relationships more pleasant and harmonious.

All obstacles get dissolved. All projects succeed. My six crystal globes smoothes the way forward, causing whatever obstacles that may manifest, or which has manifested, to quickly dissolve. These crystal balls also engender a sense of harmony in the home, causing all family members to be tolerant of one another. It really makes for great harmony and loving energy in the home.

I place several three-inch diameter crystal globes on coffee tables around the house basically to enhance the goodwill between everyone living here. This ensures no hostilities between me and my husband and ensures my staff also do not fight with me, or with one another.

There is instead a discernible pervasive air of harmony that is both gentle and heartwarming. As a result, we enjoy a truly good relationship with our domestic help as well as with those who work with us in the business. Solid crystal balls are perfect for grounding the energy of houses; in my home, I never forget this, which is why merely having the smaller globes even in multiples of six is definitely insufficient to satisfy me.

I have in fact also invested in several very large crystal balls, and these exude a warm and very welcoming esoteric presence in my home. The larger crystal balls are useful for heightening the protective element. In recent years, I have added the spiritual dimension by having powerful mantras and prayers etched onto the crystal balls. Placed amongst the other crystals, these bring empowering energy that blesses the home further.

Top: **A large sized crystal ball with Mother Tara and her mantra etched onto it.**

Above: **Another cluster of crystal balls I have in my home. These ones have exquisite artwork painted onto the inside by hand.**

Solid crystal balls are perfect for grounding the energy of houses; in my home, I never forget this, which is why merely having the smaller globes even in multiples of six is definitely insufficient to satisfy me.

Facing Page: **Pictured here are a pair of crystal apples with a beautiful Kwan Yin made of porcerlain.**

Glass Apples
symbolizing
peace in the home

I have also placed a couple of crystal and glass apples by my front door as you enter the house. These small little apples are reminiscent of New York where I lived for a short while during the mid-seventies – they call New York the big apple, so the coloured glass apples on my coffee table – in addition to their feng shui significance – also serves to remind me of a very happy time of my life, the years when I was a graduate student at Harvard B School, and when I spent so much of my free time in New York. These glass apples bring peace and harmony into the home, but they also remind me of my happy student days in Boston.

Jack, my first grandson visits me every day, bringing pure yang chi that revitalizes the home on a continuous basis. Jack laughs and smiles alot. He is a happy child and this mirrors the energy of my home.

Left: Here is my grandson Jack, leaning onto my Dolphin table purchased when I was running Dragon Seed. We had a home & design center which sold high end Italian furniture, and this is one the pieces I picked out for myself. On top of this table are more crystal balls, these ones to improve the feng shui of the new wing where my mother lives.

PART 3
THE WONDERS OF WATER

Water, in all its permutations, plays a big part in feng shui, and having water features such as ponds, swimming pools and small waterfalls can be extremely beneficial. In fact if you want to use feng shui to improve your financial status then you definately must know about water in feng shui practice..

It is helpful to differentiate between a flow of water and a body of water; one influences income luck, while the other affects wealth accumulation and growth in one's assets. Water flows and pools must also be placed in beneficial sectors and flows of water must be in the correct direction to be effective as feng shui enhancers. Let me show you how I designed my water features.

USING WATER
to attract good old-fashioned prosperity luck

A flow of water brings income, a regular inflow of money. But income is different from wealth; just as a river is not the same as a lake or a pond.

When water collects as in a lake or a pond, then water like this represents asset wealth, a family's long term fortune.

Above: Charok Lama blessing the fish in the outdoor pond that faces my dining room. This was before we expanded our house to include 11A.

Facing Page: Keeping fish is a great way to create yang water in the home. These are my feng shui fish which live in the pond that was originally outside my home, but which moved inside after our Period of 7 renovation.

Water is the second of the two words "feng shui", the first word being Wind. Wind, together with Water, is what creates the shapes and contours of the landscape; in the process, these two forces generate landforms - mountains and water flows that together determine the quality of energy created. But while wind collects and disperses energy, water directs its flow and its accumulation, especially the accumulation of good fortune which then manifests as money luck.

The flow of water is usually a river, or it can be a canal, a stream or even a road that is lower than the land surrounding it. Roads are often regarded as conduits of flow, so these are also regarded as "water".

A flow of water brings income - a regular inflow of money. But income is different from wealth; just as a river is not the same as a lake or a pond. When water collects as in a lake or a pond, then water like this represents asset wealth, a family's long term fortune.

Natural water flows and lakes created by the forces of nature are far more potent in terms of feng shui strength and when one's house can be successfully oriented to "capture" the good feng shui of natural flowing or naturally collected water, the wealth luck created is said to be exceptional. This is because natural water is usually mountain water which represents the forces of nature created over thousands of years. Herein lies its power. When energy is compressed for so many thousands of years, and then released, its potency is incredibly powerful.

But it is not easy to capture the good feng shui of natural water; so for city dwellers like me, with access to relatively small areas of land, well, people like me and most of us, we have to depend on man-made water flows and man-made accumulations of water. And while these may have only a tiny percentage of the potency of the real thing, nevertheless, good prosperity feng shui brought by man-made water features can be incredibly awesome; especially when the water flow is correctly oriented, and the pond or pool of water is correctly positioned.

In feng shui terms, this means adhering as correctly as possible to the different compass formulas that deal with using water to bring wealth luck. Hence water features and flows specially built to serve a feng shui purpose can and does work, as it has been my great good fortune to observe all these years.

Implicit in living with good feng shui is the incorporation of luck-bringing water in the home.

For me, I have worked at creating correct water flows to ensure a **steady inflow of income**, as well as wealth-enhancing ponds and pools that safeguard my **long term fortune**. I thus make sure that my good feng shui delivers both kinds of wealth luck, a steady inflow of income and a steady appreciation and expansion of my family wealth. We are traditional in our thinking - we want to leave our children and grandchildren with something substantial after we are long gone.

Southwest Swimming Pool

This is the most important water feature in my house and from the start of the book, I have made references to it, explaining its tremendous feng shui significance in bringing excellent money luck for me and my family.

There are several important reasons why this water feature is doing multiple duty here, so just to quickly recap, I will list the important feng shui significance of this wonderful pool of water, which is deep and large, making it a very substantial feng shui enhancer.

The basics of water feng shui are well taken care. You will see that the water is kept very clean, so clean that you can see the figure 8 at the bottom of the pool. Water is made to flow inwards towards the main door, so this symbolizes money flowing in.

The water is located in the Southwest grid of the house, so it is activating the Indirect Spirit of the current period of 8. Water here therefore brings wealth until 2024.

Water at the front entrance of any home always stimulates wood element sheng chi and this brings growth luck. Note that unless one's good fortune continues to grow, there will be stagnation, and that is when negative influences start to undermine your luck. This uses the *Eight Mansions* formula of feng shui. Water here also activates my Water Star 8 which is located exactly where the pool is located. This is based on *Flying Star* feng shui.

To make the water here even more auspicious, I have decorated it with a pantheon of Buddhist and Taoist deities, and there are also marble and porcelain dragons to strengthen the energy of the water.

About a year ago, I also built a **Prayer Wheel** near the pool and this serves to bless the pool's waters each time I turn the prayer wheel. Needless to say, when I swim in the pool, which I do at least three times a week, I also feel very blessed by the very auspicious water.

Kuan Yin Nectar

Inside the Southwest pool is a specially made white Kuan Yin statue from whose little wu lou - which she holds in her left hand - comes a continuous flow of blessing nectar which goes into the pool, mingles with the water in there, then flows towards the house.

For me personally, this has great significance; this is something I have always dreamed of having a Kuan Yin in exactly this posture, pouring nectar from a wu lou, keeping us healthy, granting us long life and keeping us blessed.

Her other hand is in the powerful action mudra which has the little finger and the index finger held up and all other fingers down. This action mudra is extremely powerful. You will find that many standing Kuan Yins have this hand gesture; and indeed, I have also noticed that many other Buddhas also use this same hand gesture.

When both hands have this mudra and the index and little fingers are joined in front of you, it is said to help you diagnose what is wrong in hard-to-feng shui houses. I myself have used this method quite frequently in some of my larger consultations, and it is really wonderful in helping you see things which you at first missed.

Thirsty Dragons
enhance the power of water to bring wealth

The two lovely white marble Dragons placed by my pool are meant to signify thirsty Dragons getting a drink at the water's edge. Taoists believe that water ponds have little power to bring wealth luck, and therefore less feng shui significance, unless they are visited by Dragons.

So I have been told that placing dragons by my water features is the one sure way of activating the power of water. This used to be quite a secret amongst Taoist feng shui masters. These days, of course, nothing is secret anymore...

Above: **A beautiful statue of Kuan Yin pours nectar from her wu lou into the pool, so every time we swim in the pool, it is like swimming in blessed nectar!**

Right: **Two marble Dragons placed by my pool signify thirsty Dragons getting a drink at the water's edge.**

Big Koi Pond

I built a very large and deep pond to house our prized Japanese carps, some of which have been with us since we moved in. The carp have seen several homes. They started life in our first pond which was built outside the house and then got moved inside, so that now, it is inside the house.

But when the carp got too large for the pond, I built them a larger pond outside the house on the West side. I built the pond against the boundary wall in the Northwest side of the house and incorporated a fall of water spewing out from the wall. This was very auspicious as it caused water to flow towards the house…

When we bought the next door property, I had to demolish this pond as we wanted to merge the two properties and the wall was being taken down. That was when the present carp pond got built, and it is fronting my guest house, because this was the most convenient place to have a pond this size.

The feng shui significance of this pond is that it is auspicious to have water at the front of the house. But it does also serve an aesthetic value, especially as we can place my very large Kuan Yin statue here as well.

By now, you know that I love placing a Kuan Yin image near water. I believe it is very auspicious of course, so ALL my pools and ponds have a Kuan Yin statue. The one here is the largest of all, as it is over ten feet tall. This is my pride and joy as it truly adds so much to the ambience of my outdoors…

Inside the pond I have placed two oxygenators which serve to send bubbles shooting from the floor of the pond. This creates an extremely auspicious simulation of water coming from a spring in the ground. This signifies water from deep within the earth coming up to the surface, making it very lucky water indeed.

Every time I recommend this to friends, they almost always have a great story to tell about its effectiveness in enhancing their financial situation. And it's so easy - just get these oxygenators from any fish shop…

Keeping carp also has a feng shui significance, as carp are known as the fish of abundance. The Chinese are especially fond

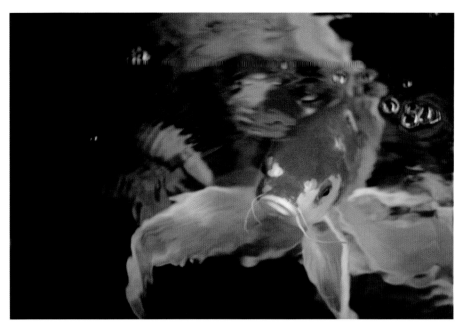

Above: **One of my beautiful carp fishes coming to the surface to say hello.**

Keeping carp has a feng shui significance because to the Chinese, the carp is a fish that signifies abundance.

of carp as they are popular symbols of good fortune.

As someone who has kept fish all my life, let me say that carp are also the easiest fish to maintain because they are so hardy and tough. Other kinds of fish can be quite difficult and when you watch them die because of wrong pH balance in the water or because there is insufficient oxygen or because the pond is infested with some bacteria… that is when it can be really heartbreaking.

Once, many years ago, when we inadvertently added some new fish into the pond and did not then know how to change half the water and add some bags of salt, which caused the older fish to die… that was when we had to watch, feeling terribly impotent and helpless, as one by one, nine of our most beautiful big, long-tailed carps just died in front of our eyes!

I cried and cried then and prayed so hard for the dying to stop… which it did eventually, because by then we had called in the experts from the fish shop, and they knew what to do. So there is plenty to learn when you keep fish for feng shui reasons. Just don't get too attached to your fish!

But if you have to go through what I went through - watching as your fish die on you - there is no need to fret about bad luck.

When your pet fish die, it does not mean bad luck at all. If anything, they probably warded off whatever bad luck might have been coming your way, by dying! But it is good to say a prayer for those that die. They cannot pray for themselves, not knowing how, but you can pray for them to have a better rebirth…

The Indoor Pond

The main water feature inside the home is the indoor pond which has great significance for us. It has been part of the house from the very start, although it started life as a garden pond. When we did decide to bring it indoors by building around it, literally embracing it, that was when we started getting wealthier, accumulating assets and for me, climbing the success and prosperity ladder by leaps and bounds.

We brought the pond in against the advice of feng shui Masters who visited us - I thought at that time it was strange that every one of them claiming to be expert in feng shui advised us so strongly against having a deep water feature inside the house.

The advice made no sense to us, so my husband and I decided to follow our own feeling. In our research on feng shui, we had discovered that wrapping the home around a body of water was one of the secrets of attaining wealth luck with feng shui... and I also instinctively felt that it was right to do so. It is now almost twenty years since we brought this pond into the home. That was when we did our first major expansion of the home after my return from living in Hong Kong... and time has proved our decision was very definitely the correct one.

We have greatly prospered since bringing the pond in... and not just in terms of having more money, but also in growing much closer as a family unit. Our daughter successfully graduated from Cambridge University, established her own successful business, fell in love, got married and very happily for us has since produced two grandsons.

Feng shui for me has thus never been about methods or formulas per se – it is about their correct application, and in this, common sense must play a big role. For us, the proof of the pudding is in the eating, and we rarely if ever make big changes to our feng shui unless we both feel comfortable doing so.

In this respect, I am lucky because my husband reads and writes Chinese, and the Chinese he learned was the old school type, under old-style teachers. It involved a great deal of memorizing of classical words which youngsters of today are not familiar with. These days they teach modern Chinese, which is in many ways an abbreviated version of the old-style words. Because of this, my husband is able to read and understand the older classical texts on

Above: **The main water feature inside our home has been with us from the start, and used to be outside until we expanded out house and brought it indoors.**

Below: **This pool has undergone several transformations. Here is the pool in 2000 before we installed a more powerful filter system in the back portion.**

feng shui. It is funny, because while he can read the texts and translate to me, he does not understand the feng shui concept being explained, while I, who do not understand classical Chinese, can.

I fully understand what he is translating mainly because my knowledge of feng shui enables me to catch the essence of what is being explained. In this respect, the authentic text books from Hong Kong and China can be very long-winded and complicated, but they are also invaluable for getting the extra dimension to understanding the formulas.

Discussions with my husband about key interpretations of compass feng shui methods have definitely helped very much in broadening my perspectives.

Goldfish Abundance

One of the things I picked up during my corporate years in Hong Kong was how much the tycoons in this city of wealthy multi-millionaires believe in the power of good feng shui. Few will admit to consulting the feng shui man, but I know they all do… and one of the things they are all very big on is keeping gold fish.

Almost every Chinese banker I visited to "pay my respects" to and introduce myself when I took over as CEO of **Dao Heng Bank** in 1982 in Hong Kong was to pay courtesy calls on my counterparts heading the other banks, local as well as international.

Banking is very much about cooperating with one another and few people realize how close-knit the banking community can be. We depend very much on the interbank market and that is because all banks are supposed to 'close' their open position at the end of each day. This means there are no outstanding liabilities. As such, we always help each other out to ensure that we are able to balance our financial positions and square off all accounts each day.

So the relationship you have with other banks is incredibly important. Because of this, one of the first things I did after taking over at Dao Heng Bank was to call on other bankers, introduce myself and basically make friends and let them know about the Group I represented. In doing the rounds, I also had the chance to observe many different offices, and believe me, nearly all of them have beautifully kept and well-maintained goldfish aquariums, if not inside

their office then definitely somewhere in the CEO's suite of offices. Some of them keep their aquariums in their board rooms, others in the foyer of the visitors' area, and still others in the inner sanctum of their office.

I discovered that the fat, slow moving goldfish was a great favourite. Goldfish signify big abundance and the way they swim - slowly and with a great deal of wiggly movement - is supposed to attract plenty of wealth luck. In fact, the gold fish is supposed to represent the slow but sure buildup of family wealth, so they were very popular with banks and companies that were majority owned by families.

I picked up my preference for goldfish from those days, and since then, although we love carps - more my husband than me - personally, I have a great preference for goldfish. But they are not as easy to nurture as the carps. It took me several months and quite a number of failed attempts before I finally succeeded in keeping them happy, frolicking and alive. In fact, I was so unsuccessful that eventually I was forced to concede defeat. I moved them all out to the North pond outside and here in the indoor pond, I kept red feng shui fish instead. These not only survived, they are thriving!

I have upgraded this part of the house many times now and in the current period, I have transformed my indoor pond area to become a special altar dedicated to Tara, the Goddess regarded as the Mother of all the Buddhas. So this part of the house has become a very special spiritual area where I keep three particularly special statues, all given to me over the years by my root guru Lama Zopa Rinpoche.

Above: **Goldfish have grown to be a real favourite of mine. They are also believed to be very lucky feng shui wise.**

Goldfish signify abundance and the way they swim - slowly and with a great deal of wiggly movement - is supposed to attract plenty of wealth luck. The goldfish is said to represent the slow but sure buildup of family wealth.

Powerful Shivalingam

In this front altar area I have placed a particularly important Shivalingam – a cylindrical shaped stone object which was said to come from the banks of India's holy river, the Ganges. Shivalingams are not manmade; instead they are believed to be like the Dzi beads of Tibet, dropped from heaven and deposited by the river banks. Every Shivalingam is different in texture and design.

Mine was given to me by a very kind student of mine from Singapore, Vincent Koh, who specializes in precious esoteric items that bring powerful good luck – items such as ammonites, shivalingams, rudrakshas and so forth. Vincent gave me this Shivalingam but forgot to tell me how to display it, so for three years mine slept on a flowerbed!

Until one day, a Hindu student from Delhi came to my house, saw it lying asleep on my flower bed, gasped at its size and quality and after much ooing and aahing proceeded to educated me on the correct care of the Shivalingam. "You will need a yoni," she told me. "This is the receptacle in which the Shivalingam is placed."

She explained that Shivalingams come alive and become the essence of Lord Shiva when they are correctly placed standing up on a yoni. I am also supposed to offer it milk by pouring it over the whole shivalingam the first time it sits on the yoni!

The following year, this same student handcarried a yoni from India for me. It is truly incredible because the yoni is made of granite and it is heavy... but there it was. I can only say how powerful must be this shivalingam; indeed so powerful that it manifests the yoni it wants from India!

That was two years ago and today, the Shivalingam sits majestically in full view of both my doors. Together, the Shivalingam on its yoni is extremely powerful in attracting auspicious luck and warding off all negative developments in the life of the household in which it resides. To Indians especially, the Shivalingam is a very sacred holy object, so I treat it as such, placing it in this most important part of the home in full view of my auspicious feng shui fish!

Above: **A Shivalingam, a cylindrical shaped stone object, said to come from the banks of India's holy river, the Ganges River. This was given to me by a friend and student of mine.**

also double up as works of art. As for what I do with enhancers and protectors from past years, these I keep nicely wrapped up and stored in my store room. For articles that can be burned, I make a big garden fire and burn them. For articles I do not wish to keep, I offer them to a big river that takes them out to sea. It is really auspicious if you can cross three bridges when travelling to a river to do this, and when you are at the river, throw them into the river, over your left shoulder.

My Tortoise Pond

Toads and tortoises are essential symbols of good fortune that really should be present in any home. These are creatures associated with water, hence their affinity with wealth luck. Tortoises however also bring the added benefit of creating longevity energy and in fact, the tortoise is also credited with giving protection against premature death for everyone living in the home.

Everyone I know who has lived really long lives – well, they have tortoises in their homes. They all tell me the same thing – that their terrapins (pet tortoises) were bought as tiny pets for their children and somehow over the years, these little terrapins have grown and become sizeable tortoises... I myself have four of them and they live in my special tortoise pond behind my house. These were brought home many years ago when Jennifer was young enough to appreciate them as pets. As the years passed however, they slowly and steadily got larger and I guess they are now very much a part of the family.

At first they lived with my carp in the North pond but as they got bigger and more aggressive, I decided they had to have their own pond, separate from the fish. This too is located in the North sector of the property, so this is the perfect place for them.

Talking of tortoises, I really have to share my story of the sea tortoise, usually referred to as turtles with you. Those of you familiar with feng shui will know that the basis of the Flying Star chart and formula is the **Lo Shu Square**, which has the nine numbers placed round a nine sector grid. Legend has it that this arrangement of numbers was brought on the back of the turtle, which sailed up the shores of the **River Lo** and given to the first emperor **Fu Hsi** – and hence the square is referred to as the Lo Shu square – it is named after the River Lo.

3 Legged Toads
attracting money luck

Above: **One of my terrapins, which lives in a pond in the North sector. This terrapin lives wirh 2 other terrapins and a star tortoise, and has been with our family for over a decade now.**

As well as being related to water hence wealth, tortoises are also known to foster longevity energies and to give protection against premature death.

One of the things anyone visiting me will notice are the number of three-legged toads I have placed under sofas and tables. This is because of all the symbols of good fortune that I have experimented with; I guess this little fella has been the most reliable in attracting opportunities that bring money!

When I first started writing feng shui books, I remember that a friend from my Hong Kong days presented me with six of these cute creatures. She told me that since I believed in feng shui and had actually written books on the subject, I was sure to like her gift. I placed them all over the house, some facing in and some facing out, and some even facing out during the mornings and facing in during the evenings. Over time, I came to realize that their facing direction was immaterial to their effectiveness. But having them inside the house really did attract lots of opportunities for us and they have never stopped working.

These days I 'retire' the older toads and I keep replenishing my home with new ones. This is exactly what I do with other symbols of protection and enhancement as well - especially symbols that I use as annual cures and remedies. After a year's work, I feel their energy has weakened and it is better to use a brand new remedy or enhancer - if I like a piece too much to keep in the store room, I use incense and rock salt to reenergize them. In any case, I do not use anything beyond two years unless they

When I returned from Hong Kong, we took a family holiday to Pangkor Island, a lovely resort off the coast of Perak. The three of us had not been on holiday together for too long, and I felt we needed some serious bonding time together, so we spent 3 nights there away from the rest of the world. On the second morning, when walking along the shore, we came upon a rather large sea turtle which had somehow got washed ashore. On closer examination, however, we discovered that it was just a turtle shell... It did not occur to me then, but many years later, one day while signing books in **Harrods** in **London**, it suddenly hit me.

That was when my mind flashed back to that encounter with the turtle shell, and I realized it must have been meant as an Oracle of my future work in feng shui, because it was shortly after our holiday that I started writing my first feng shui book, and today, many years later, my books have brought me a worldwide following of students as well as a global business popularizing this living skill. Next time you encounter something significant like this, it just might be telling you something about what's in store for you...

Five Ghosts bring Gold

The most important pond in my house is the **six-tier waterfall** and pond in the North. This pond is located at the back of the house and was built in the last Period of 7. Between 1984 to 2004 (Period 7), the Water Star 8 of my house was in the North sector based on Flying Star, but this was also the sector where the **Five Ghosts** were present under the Eight Mansions method. This sector thus had the potential to bring a great deal of aggravations caused by the five ghosts – a condition that suggests us falling victim to gossip and troublemakers who create obstacles to everything we do; OR I could use my feng shui knowledge to transform the misfortune luck of five ghosts here into great good fortune known in feng shui terms as "*five ghosts bringing gold*".

I could do this during the years that fell into Period 7 because the Flying Star chart for our home then had the auspicious Water Star 8 in the North sector. I knew then that I had to build a water feature here to activate the Water Star 8. Doing this would bring us prosperity luck, and it would also transform the five ghosts misfortune into good fortune. This means that for people

Top: **The six-tier waterfall in the North sector of our home. This was built to transform the Five Ghosts affliction into "Five Ghosts Bringing Gold". The North also happened to be where my Water Star 8 was at the time, so after I arranged for this pond to be built, our fortunes improved steadily over time.**

Above: **A statue of the Lady of the Nine Heavens, the legendary lady believed to have brought the Lo Pan to the Yellow Emperor providing him the tool used to unlock all the secrets in feng shui, sits amidst my water feature in the North.**

Above: **White Dzambhala who sits on a turqoise dragon is the powerful Wealth Buddha who bestows prosperity blessings to those who offer water washing over his head. This statue, carved from a piece of granite has been in my North pond for ten years.**

who may be jealous of my success or wish me harm, somehow their bad intentions would symbolically be transformed into gold. This pond was built in 1991 and since then, the fortunes of the home have been steadily improving.

NOTE: To transform the Five Ghosts from bad into good luck, just install a waterfall there with a pond. This is even more effective if that corner happens to also carry the Water Star 8 of the current period!

But to be beneficial, it had to be a waterfall. This was because the North sector of my house was located behind, at the back of the house, which always benefits from having a "mountain" - i.e. higher ground. Any water feature built here must be a waterfall to ensure the mountain at the back of the house does not symbolically "fall into the water". If this happens, then our health luck would be negatively affected and also our relationship luck.

To make the waterfall truly auspicious, I designed a six-level waterfall as this would signify "water from heaven". It took a great deal of effort to get this waterfall right, but once we did, it went to work almost immediately, creating plenty of good fortune for us... that eventually led to my starting a career as a writer of bestselling books.

Dzambhala Waterfall

We felt the positive effects of my North pond with its fish and its waterfall almost immediately after we built it, and in its nearly eighteen years of existence, the pond has seen many changes in its fish population as well as in the way a variety of water plants have been successfully planted here. Today, the pond has matured and the plants that have taken root here have given it a character of its own. In 1997 soon after I met Lama Zopa Rinpoche, and he initiated me into the practice of offering water to the Tibetan Wealth Buddha known as the **White Dzambhala**, I have added the dimension of spiritual enhancement to the pond.

I went to Katmandu to shop for beautifully-carved stone statues of Dzambhala and placed them sitting on the steps of the waterfall, positioning them in such a way as to receive water flowing continuously on their head. This creates the auspicious water offering symbolism in your waterfall, which over time should bring you wealth luck. This is a practice known to many Tibetans; and if you can receive initiation into the practice of the Dzambhalas from a high lama who possesses the lineage, it will empower your practice even more. If you do the practice I describe below, which involves chanting the appropriate mantra, then it will create the cause for you to eventually receive just such an initiation.

Indeed, if you also know how to recite the mantras to the Dzambhala, then doing so while pouring water over Dzambhala's head will help you create wonderful affinity with the Dzambhala and this in turn will attract great wealth luck for you and your family.

For those keen on performing a meaningful daily water offering to the White Dzambhala – the Wealth Buddha that sits on a turquoise dragon and carries a trident and a staff with a mongoose in its left hand – here is the mantra which you can recite. It includes the mantra to Dzambhala followed by the mantra to the four dakinis of the four directions who all bring wealth luck with the Dzambhala.

While reciting, perform the water offering i.e. place an image of the Dzambhala on a little stand inside a crystal bowl and then slowly pour water over its head with a water jug… and visualize the Dzambhala, the mongoose and the dragon creating lots and lots of dollar bills pouring into your home. Please note that this creative visualization is very helpful to getting quick results…

Om Padma Krodha Arya
Dzambhala Hridaya Hum Peh

(recite 108 times followed by...)

Om Vajra Dakini Hum Peh,
Om Ratna Dakini Hum Peh,
Om Padma Dakini Hum Peh,
Om Karma Dakini Hum Peh,
Sarva Siddhi Hum.

(recite 28 times)

Water Flow Direction

Water feng shui in any home is incomplete if the flow of water past the main door and around the house is not correctly oriented. Unfortunately, doing this correctly requires knowledge of the water feng shui formulas and this can be quite challenging for the amateur practitioner. I have written a book

on these water formulas, but applying the formula on water can be difficult… For those who want to ensure your flow of water is correct, perhaps I can make it a little easier. What you need to do is to take note of two vital aspects to the flow of your water:

1. Any water which flows past your main door must flow either from left to right OR from right to left. This depends on the facing direction of the house. If your house faces a primary direction (i.e. North, South, East or West) then water must flow past your main door from left to right. If your house faces a secondary direction (i.e. SE, NW, SW or NE) then any flow of water past your house should flow from right to left. Since my house faces SW, the water in my drain must flow past my front door from right to left.

2. The water must then flow out of your house in an auspicious direction. This is part of the Water Formula and you can determine the auspicious exit direction of water for your house. Mine was for the water to exit in a South direction, so I had to build my drains to accommodate this.

Building the drains correctly is something of a challenge, so I decided to make it easy for myself. I have known the first rule of water flow since when the house was built. For us, the slope of the road outside the house slopes downwards from left to right, so our land naturally flowed this way. This meant that natural water would also flow this direction, which is inauspicious for my house. So first I had to completely block out views of the outside flow of water.

This meant building a wall to block all views of the outside drain. It took us some time to get this done in the Seventies… those were days when we had to be very mindful of our budget. But soon after the wall got built and my water flow was then correctly flowing past my SW (secondary direction) facing door, my career just took off! That was how I landed a dream job with the Hong Leong group! The correct flow of water brought me stunning career luck.

I was also very careful to orientate the exit direction of drain water correctly, and to this day, the exit drain still works great for us. Because the formula is so difficult to implement, my exit direction is only about 3 ft long. After that, the rest of the drain is kept closed. This effectively "taps" the correct direction.

Any water which flows past your main door - be it a domestic drain, a larger monsoon drain outside the house, a canal or a river - must either flow from left to right, or right to left.

If your house faces a primary direction, then water should flow past from left to right. If your house faces a secondary direction, then the water should flow past from right to left.

PART 4
DINING AUSPICIOUS

This part of the home is where family members interact the most with each other, and the feng shui here should aim at creating harmony and goodwill within the family. Food is also symbolic of the family's asset wealth, so I go to great lengths to ensure that our dining areas are designed to attract both harmony and prosperity luck, with each member of the family sitting facing their best direction, and with the proper enhancers in place to ensure good fortune for everyone.

EATING WELL
where the family eats is most important

The most important thing to display in the dining room are the Three Star Gods - Fuk Luk Sau, revered by the Chinese because they represent health, wealth & happiness.

Above: **I usually like to have a basket of fresh fruit in the dining room area. This signifies abundance.**

There are three dining areas in my house, but the one we use the most is the family dining area which is located in the inner half of the home adjacent to the kitchen at the back. This is where we spend most of our time... eating, chatting, discussing our day, our work and planning our holidays and our overseas trips. Almost everything we do starts at the dining table from breakfast through lunch and into dinner. So for me, dining auspicious is something I take as given. We must generate good luck every time we sit down to eat.

I consider myself incredibly lucky because Jennifer eats at least one meal with me every day. She lives two houses away from us, so each morning we use our breakfast time to discuss business before she goes to work at the office and I go into my home workplace to attend to emails and do my writing.

So in terms of the amount of time we spend here, the dining area is really important, and I make sure the feng shui here is always auspicious. This family dining area is not large, but it is the focal point of our home. Here, the visual views from the table where we eat and chat are important as these create subconscious mental images that influence our frame of mind. I subscribe to the view that as long as we are always happy, joking and enjoying each other when we eat, we cannot go far wrong in the harmony stakes. And good feng shui always begins with a harmonious home.

The most important display item here is **Fuk Luk Sau**, the Three Star Gods revered by the Chinese because they symbolize health, wealth and prosperity. Implicit in the presence of Fuk Luk Sau is protection against premature death (which means longevity luck), protection against serious illness, plenty of good fortune that include success and wealth luck, and harmony luck in all our relationships, with one another and with others.

The presence of these Three Star Gods is vital and to Chinese families who believe in feng shui, these deities signify their inner aspirations. They are not worshipped as religious deities but are respected as the spiritual and cosmic representations of every person's inner desires. Having their presence in the dining area ensures that when the family sits down to dine they receive good chi from these deities. In my family dining room, to make sure everyone has a good view of Fuk Luk Sau, I actually have two lovely sets facing us. Both sets are large and grand looking, colourful and very well crafted.

One set is placed on a sideboard inside the home facing Northeast, the sitting direction of the house, and another set is placed overlooking the North pond outside and facing Southeast. Thus I have one set of Fuk Luk Sau facing a West group direction (to benefit me) and another set facing an East group direction (benefiting my husband and my daughter).

As a result, the happy smiles of these deities which are so important in feng shui are well embedded inside my head. There is also a powerful *Taoist belief in the concept of double goodness* so it is excellent to have not one, but two, of anything auspicious.

Fuk Luk Sau benefits everyone so I have encouraged all my friends to invite them into their homes. They benefit any household that has them and in fact there are additional sets (but smaller) in other parts of my home as well – wherever we dine or entertain guests. These are made of carved crystal, wood sculptures and of porcelain or brass. It is safe to say that Fuk Luk Sau signifies the manifestation of good feng shui and if a set is given to you by your parents, it is even more auspicious, as this means that the older generation passes on genuine good fortune to you.

Above: Fuk Luk Sau, the Three Star Gods, are displayed on a sideboard table where they can be seen when we sit down at the dining table.

Left: Sometimes our main family dining table becomes a buffet spread when we throw a party or have friends over.

Family Dining
with Mirror Wall

In keeping with the theme of double goodness, we have installed a very large wall mirror in the dining area. This directly reflects the food served on the table and has the effect of doubling everything placed on the table, thereby generating a feeling of abundance and plenty.

The Chinese place great emphasis on food and it is incredibly important for the family to always eat with lots of food on the table and to have this reflected as well.

Large families who do not live together should eat together as often as possible – at least once a week. We believe that *the family that eats together stays together* and I know that many of the wealthy dynastic type families in Hong Kong make it a point to have at least one meal together – usually held on a Sunday to ensure everyone can make it.

This is when feelings of warmth and goodwill are generated. There should be at least three generations at this meal to make it really auspicious for family harmony and wellbeing. Needless to say, in my family we follow this tradition faithfully, so Sunday lunch is family time for us. However, we do not necessarily have to eat at home all the time and we do not – we use this opportunity to try out all the latest new restaurants in town!

When you have a wall mirror in your dining room, it not only reflects the food on the table, it also "locks" in all the moments when the family is happily eating together... this has the effect of ensuring the family stays together, **the father and mother do not split up** and most importantly, **the siblings in the family look out for one another** rather than fight (perhaps over the family fortune). Ensuring harmony amongst siblings must start from a very young age and it always begins at the dining table.

Please do make sure however, that should you decide to have a mirror wall in your dining area, that you make it high enough so no one's head gets "cut off" in the reflection. It should be high enough to reflect the tallest member of the family but also low enough to reflect the feet. Neither the head nor the

Main Picture: **It is always good to have a wall mirror next to the dining table to reflect the food - this adheres to the concept of double goodness. But it is always better to have one big mirror than to have mirror tiles, as the fragmented reflection given off by the tiles does not have such a good symbolic meaning.**

feet should get cut off. Half mirrors that are placed just above the sideboard are also acceptable, but these should reflect the heads of everyone in the room. And talking about mirrors, please do NOT place mirrors inside the kitchen.

I remember how appalled I was when I once did a consultation for a woman in London who had invited what I call a *feng shui junkie* into her home who advised her to place mirror tiles along her kitchen walls "to double the food being cooked." What she did not know was that her mirror tiles were

actually reflecting the fire. No wonder she suffered from so much misfortune luck after doing that. Once she removed the mirror tiles, her life returned to normal, so do use a discerning mind whenever you are told to do anything. Think through whatever advice is being given to you. Unless what I (or anyone else says) makes sense in the context of your home, you do not need to follow the advice blindly. Feng shui is also common sense.

Meanwhile, talking about **mirror tiles**, I am so against these because they actually cause a great deal of bad feng shui to occur.

Mirror tiles basically distort the reflections of people walking in the home, and when placed in the dining area, they cause disruptions to your income, your wealth and your well being.

Mirror tiles in the living area cause hostility to occur amongst family members and between you and people who come and visit you. If you want to enjoy double goodness using mirrors, it is best to invest in large pieces of mirrors that cover an entire wall. Make the reflective surface a feature wall and have it beveled as well,

as this in effect creates a nice looking frame for all the things and people it reflects. It is also advisable to use good mirrors that do not distort your reflection, neither making you look fatter or thinner. And to keep mirrors clean and clear, wipe them with dry newspaper rather than wet cloth!

Circular Table

An important feature of the family dining area is that **a round table is preferred** over a rectangular or square table. It is the circular table that brings harmony feng shui to members of the family. Square tables create four sides with four pointed edges, and these are not as auspicious as circular tables.

The round shape signifies heaven energy, and combines with **square rooms** and the human element to create the trinity of *tien ti ren* – heaven, earth and mankind energy. Creating this trinity is the key that unlocks loads of beneficial feng shui. *Tien ti ren* is actually the secret component in effective feng shui practice.

For these reasons, I have always used round dining tables. I used to have a rosewood table seating eight people that was beautifully inlaid with mother of pearl images, but this table eventually proved too small for our growing family, so I moved it to my entertaining area where I have two other tables, and replaced it with a lovely yellow marble table that seats twelve. The change has proved very beneficial in that my "extended" family – my nephew and my niece and their families – has since become much closer. As the family matriarch, this makes me very happy and fulfilled.

I selected **yellow marble** because this signifies **Earth** which combines well with the **Heaven** luck of the circular shape. My dining area is not square, and to create the trinity of *tien ti ren*, I needed to strengthen the energy of Earth; so now all my extended family members fit comfortably.

In keeping with the concept of double goodness, I have a matching **lazy susan** which rotates around the table. This makes it easier for food to be within reach of everyone, but more importantly, it actively energizes the double goodness of heaven luck. A moving center piece also creates active chi on the table itself. This is so beneficial because it ensures the chi is always fresh and always activated.

Not many people know this, but letting the *lazy susan* move in a counter-clockwise direction makes it more empowering and effective for ensuring excellent heaven luck; this is better than letting it move round in a clockwise direction. Heaven luck brings sudden windfalls into your life, unexpected good fortune which comes when you least expect it! For those of you in business or those taking risks with their money, heaven luck is really important to have!

To facilitate a **good feng shui sitting arrangement**, the compass orientations are clearly indicated so that everyone can sit according to whether they are East or West group people. I advise them that it is not necessary to sit facing their personal sheng chi direction when eating with your family; in fact, it is advisable not to do so, as that just makes you more competitive. Better to sit facing your *nien yen* direction which fosters harmony and goodwill. This is according to the *Eight Mansions* formula of personalized lucky directions derived from one's date of birth.

Wealth Pot

In the center of my big round dining table, I have placed a wealth pot filled with money at the bottom and plenty of faux golden ingots, gemstones and other emblems of good fortune. Here the yellow colour of our wealth pot signifies plenty of abundance. It can also symbolize *Earth element* energy. As a result, the theme of heaven and earth is brought into play and these two aspects of the cosmic forces marries with *mankind* (us!) to create the trinity that is so vital to generating good feng shui. This is the essence of feng shui, which must be present before good fortune can manifest.

The concept of the wealth pot is not unlike the wealth vase, but while the vase is closed up and hidden deep inside the home, the wealth pot is excellent when displayed on the dining table; or on the coffee table in the living area. The wealth pot signifies the aspiration of the family to become wealthy,

Above: **A wealth pot sits in the center of my main dining table. In it are gemstones, ingots and other emblems of good fortune. The Buddha Maitreya - the future Buddha - takes center stage.**

Facing Page: **Rosewood dining table with mother of pearl inlay is reflected in the wall mirror of my dining room. Each time we sit down for a meal, the food gets reflected and symbolically doubled, signifying abundance.**

Above: A complete set of offerings is shown above. These are meant for the extensive Hayagriva Fire Puja which I had performed in our home just after 11A was completed. This was a purification puja.

Below: Picture shows Geshe Deyang leading the fire puja.

so it should be filled with money and emblems of wealth.

I put nine currencies hidden deep under a pile of "old' ingots into mine, and naturally, I make sure I only put good solid currencies. In recent years, I have been very much enamored of the Chinese *renminbi* and the European Euro. In fact, for this period of 8, all currencies that have two horizontal lines cutting across are auspicious. These include the Chinese currency, the Euro and the Yen – these are currencies that will always have a value. Never put banana money into your wealth pot.

My beautiful wealth pot rotates on a special stand. It is yellow in colour, in a shade that is both pleasing and auspicious, and it is made of porcelain; truly a work of art with the colours so well glazed and so perfectly fired that it stands out. Just looking at it makes me feel great!

Seated on the ingots inside the wealth pot is beautiful Maitreya Buddha, the future Buddha. This statue was given to me by my root guru, Lama Zopa Rinpoche, and this is the exact replica of the statue which Rinpoche is trying to build – very, very big – in Bodhgaya in India! He has spoken to me so many times about how important it is to build the Maitreya statue in India that I feel it is definitely auspicious to have Maitreya presiding over my dining table sitting on a wealth pot, reminding me every day about this message from Rinpoche.

Inside the wealth pot I have also placed many small figurines of the Rooster and this signifies my inner aspiration to be able to help big time in building this statue, if not in this life time then in the next. Dining feng shui is well and good, but it is incredibly beneficial to introduce the all-important element of spiritual aspirations into the dining experience as well.

Daily Food Offering

Indeed, one of the rituals at my dining table is that of offering food to the Buddhas and Bodhisattvas – a practice not unlike that of saying grace before eating. But the Buddhist practice of praying before eating is mainly to invoke blessings and to offer the food to one's gurus as well. We believe there is immense karmic merit in remembering to make food offerings three times a day, as this serves to remind us how blessed and lucky we are to be able to sit down every day with more than enough to eat.

More than offering food however, I have also been advised by many high lamas that making what the Tibetan Buddhists refer to as **Tsog Offerings** is even more auspicious and creates huge merit. There is this special Tsog offering prayer which was translated many years ago into English. It is very rare and it was passed to me by an American nun, who has done more than 12 years of solitary retreat. She was living in Rinpoche's house at Aptos in California at that time and I was doing a seven day Green Tara retreat there.

It was 1998 a year after I had met Lama Zopa Rinpoche, who had asked her to help me do the retreat, teach me the ropes, so to speak and she was really wonderful. Because of her, I succeeded in making a life-long connection with Tara, the Goddess regarded by many to be the mother of all the Tathagatas, the mother of all the Buddhas…

Her name was Venerable Paula and at the end of the seven days, she shared this Tsog Offering prayer with me. She said it had been given to her by the late **Kirti Tsenshab Rinpoche**, a very highly realized lama who had lived in **Dharamsala** for many years and who passed away recently.

I have been using this prayer offering since then, especially after Lama Zopa heard me doing it one time and he has told me to do it each time we eat together. I knew then that this Tsog Offering prayer was mighty special... so here it is. I am really happy to share it with you. If you like it, copy it and use it to bless your food each time you sit down to eat.

There are two parts to the Offering Prayer, first the blessing mantra which is in Tibetan and multiplies the merit of making the offering a million times and then comes the offering in English. Recite the entire prayer once through and then dedicate the merit to whatever it is you wish for. More than good feng shui, doing this prayer offering will invoke a shower of blessings for you and your family.

Food Offering Mantra

OM NAMO BHAGAVATE BENDZAY SARWA PARMA
DANA, TATHAGATAYA ARHATE/
SAMYAK SAM BUDDHAYA TAYATA OM BENDZAY
BENDZAY/

MAHA BENDZAY / MAHA TAYDZA BENDZAY /
MAHA BIDYA BENDZAY /
MAHA BODHICITTA BENDZAY / MAHA BODHI MENDO
PASAM KRAMANA BENDZAY /
SARWA KARMA AWARANA BISHO DANA
BENDAZAY SOHA.
(3 times)

EM AH HO / EM AH HO / EM AH HO

Food, Drink, five meat, five nectar, that which is in the skull, while it is
in the nature of bliss and voidness, purified, actualized, increased by
the three Vajras it became oceans of uncontaminated nectar.

OM AH HUM / OM AH HUM / OH AH HUM

Dharmachakra, center of the heart, Indestructible subtle wind and
mind, Inseparable from supreme merit field, assemblies of gurus & mind
sealed deities, I offer desire enjoyment of the circle of the Tsog. In
the state of great bliss please take by being pleased and satisfied.
Please grant blessings to achieve in this life the unified mahamudra of
the profound vajra yoga, that which is inseparable with method and
wisdom.

My Wall of Tsa Tsas

As soon as I started making daily Tsog Offerings, I felt increasingly inspired by the profound and great meaning behind doing it. I recall, in the early years of the new millennium, how impressed I was by Rinpoche's vast knowledge of Buddhism and how pure his heart and motivations always were.

I also loved the non-judgemental way he taught Buddhism and how easy he made it for me, and for his thousands of disciples. Most of all, I identified with the way Rinpoche simplified the practices, as a result of which my house now resonates with the teachings I have absorbed over the past ten years.

Above: **Facing my dining table is a wall of TsaTsas, which are miniature images of Buddha Deities done by us.**

Instinctively, I incorporate the merit-making practices I learnt from Rinpoche with my own knowledge of feng shui symbolism and Taoist rituals, as a result of which my home is now a seamless mix of the two great philosophies that also influenced China's cultural development – Taoism and Buddhism – except that in my home, the influence of our own contemporary times is always pervasive. Mine is a modern home that is heavily influenced by ancient traditions.

I felt that making my food offerings each day would be more meaningful if I had images of the Buddhas and Bodhisattvas I was making the offerings to. By then, we had also mastered the fine art of making tsa tsa – these are tiny miniature Buddha statues made of plaster from rubber moulds bought from **Nalanda monastery** in **France**.

In no time at all, after the French monk **Ven. Jean Francoise** from Nalanda came to stay with me and taught us how, we could now make tsa tsas; and since Malaysia has a wonderful source of amazingly good plaster clay (from the limestone hills of Ipoh) we started making tsa tsas of every Buddha I knew, and whose mould was easily made available for me by the monks of Nalanda monastery in France.

Before long, I had filled all the nooks and corners of my ceilings with tsa tsas… and in my dining area I created a **Wall of Buddhas** made entirely of tsa tsas. After that it really became meaningful making my food offerings and when Rinpoche first laid eyes on my tsa tsa wall and my tsa tsa ceilings, he was so pleased he gave me such a compliment that in one of those rare moments in my life, I blushed.

Chandelier Brightness as we dine

Above the dining table is a flat chandelier that hangs from a rather low wooden ceiling. This is my original ceiling and this part of the house is low. In those days when we first built this house, we did not have the budget to have large rooms or high ceilings, so what we did was just to build a house that cost as much as we could afford, although here and there is evidence of our indulgences.

The wooden ceiling then was very in vogue, because hard wood was quite expensive, and this is the reason my husband and I are reluctant to change the wooden ceiling even though it makes the house rather dark. Instead, we have installed the bright lights of the chandelier.

We also use warm light bulbs as this creates a much better ambience, and our chandelier comprises plenty of rounded and faceted crystals, which multiply the amount of light emanating outwards. This is the main reason why I like chandeliers. I love the reflections of crystals inside the house. They send out radiating light which is always auspicious.

In feng shui, bright lights are one of the most effective ways of waking up the energy of any space. In fact, lights work as well as if not better than movement and sound, the other two effective methods of energizing space. In the dining area, bright lights are excellent feng shui. It is ALWAYS better eating in bright light than eating in dim light.

Thus I have never subscribed to the idea of candlelit dining. I like to see what I eat. In any case, the Chinese do not equate dim-light dining with abundance and wealth, nor with romance. The emperors in the old days always dined in rooms that were brightly lit with thousands of candles… while the poor always dined in dimly lit rooms. Hence if you want abundance, make sure the lighting in your dining area is more than adequate. Lights should never be glaring but should be warm, and they should allow you to see clearly.

All Kinds of Lighting

I also use spotlights and halogens for focused and spot lighting. The tiny halogens are great for creating mood lighting in the home. Especially when I am eating by myself, I like the room to be bright but not glaring. That is when I turn on my halogen lighting. These create amazingly powerful Fire element energy in a muted way. I find they are incredibly effective in sending down slivers of light that have the effect of beams of light radiating downwards, while spotlights shine more directly.

I use different lighting for different symbols of good fortune which vary from year to year. Also, different sectors of the dining room need extra focus in different years. As such, I find it really beneficial to have movable spot lighting that can do the job of activating powerful feng shui enhancers and cures.

Making light offerings to the holy art that hang on my walls is something I take very seriously. These are thangkas – paintings of Buddhas and Bodhisattvas – that grace almost every wall of my home.

The beauty of these great thangkas can only come into focus when a bright light shines directly at them, and it is then that the gold that is painted (as offerings to the holy objects that are the subject matter of the art) are revealed in sharp focus, and that is when the paintings hanging on my walls become magical.

In feng shui, bright lights are one of the most effective ways of waking up the energy of any space.

Over the years I have been very fortunate in finding some exceptional pieces. These hang in the public areas of my home in great splendour. In the dining area, a very exquisite appliquéd thangka of the three faced Buddha of Longevity, **Nyamglyma**, hangs on the Northwest wall, and it showers down a rain of powerful blessings. This is one of the more prominent walls in my home, hence I reserved this spot for Namglyma.

I also use what the architects call wall washes. This successfully creates indirect lighting that produce the effect of daytime ambience during the night, very similar to having yin and yang energy while eating irrespective of whether one is eating lunch or dinner. For this, we use white light, and here, the bulbs are never seen. Instead, light is created using hidden fluorescent bulbs.

Irrespective of what kind of lighting is used, brightness always creates good fortune yang chi. The use of lights can be either as a cure or as an enhancer. It depends very much on how the light is used, and on whether it is warm, yellow light or cold, white light.

24 Hour TV News

Living with good feng shui in the 21st century must reflect the amazing scientific advances of our times. We live in an age when news travels fast, and there is worldwide global connectivity that creates its own brand of energy. So it is really vital for us to be on top of the news at all hours of the day and night.

As a result, I do not stint on TV sets, and in our home, there as many television sets as there are rooms, and everyone is connected to all the channels available here. I subscribe to the concept that to live auspiciously, we must live in sync with all the advances of our Age. This signifies prosperity more than just money in the bank.

So there is a TV in the dining area to make sure that should there be any special news announcement, we do not miss it. The TV basically brings the world into our dining room. I cannot count the number of times when breaking news happened even as we ate; the 9/11 disaster that happened in New York unfolded even as we ate dinner; the death of princess Diana; the tsunami that crashed into so many Indian Ocean countries and bringing so much sufferings also occurred while we were having a meal… but we also do not want to miss any of our must-watch shows such as the amazing show put on by Beijing for the Olympics in 2008, and of course American Idol which always come on over prime time – which is dinner time!

> Having the television turned on adds movement & sound to the dining area and **this generates good power forces as well**. Movement suggests plenty of mankind energy present and this combines beautifully with the heaven and earth energy created by the dining table.

Hence we are never short of the *tien ti ren* trinity in our dining area. The essence of good fortune chi is always present every time we sit down to eat. In this connection, I have to say that eating must be a time of goodwill, hence it is really bad luck to quarrel or be hostile during mealtimes. This is the best time for the family members to bond with each other, spend quality time exchanging ideas, and catching up with one another's activities.

Symbolic Abundance

To add to the dining room ambience, it is also important for any family to create a sense of abundance. There should always be plenty of food on the table and absolutely no suggestion at all of anything missing.

Even when there are just the two of you eating, it is a good idea to arrange the food in such a way that there is a feeling of abundance. The presence of a full table supported by a full pantry and refrigerator is what creates the energy of plenty in any

home. Try to never run out of the staples in your home. Foodstuff such as rice, bread, sugar and other basic items must be available in the home at all times. This is how I manage the domestic side of my existence. I take an active role in making certain there is always more than enough food not just for me and my family but also for unexpected guests, for my dogs and for my fish.

In short, this is a house that must never run out of food. I faithfully create this state of symbolic abundance at all times. So you will never hear me talk about food wastage, because I believe in always serving more than anyone can eat, especially when there are guests dining with me.

In this, I reflect the popular tradition amongst Chinese to always have a full table. This is what creates good prosperity feng shui. Meanwhile, none of the plates and glasses used should be chipped or have cracks. Throw these away as using them creates the feng shui of obstacles blocking your success. Eating from a cracked plate or bowl is also considered a sign that you will have your rice bowl broken – this means losing your job, or if you are business, causing your business to go bust.

When you drink from a broken tea cup, it is even more serious, since this signifies a betrayal by someone close to you, a betrayal which can easily cause you mental anguish that leads to illness. So I freak out if a chipped teacup or glass is ever used to serve anything to me or my family members. In the same vein, broken cooking pots or utensils should also be thrown away. To cook from anything broken is the height of inauspiciousness.

Below: I keep open house for all my relatives who should visit more frequently actually, and when they do, the dining room gets energized and there are always yummy goodies on the table. This picture shows my uncles visiting me for tea.

View of
Outdoors Water

Our family dining area opens out to the outdoors, facing Northwest but looking directly at the North pond which currently houses my beautiful goldfish. The **White Dzambhala Tibetan Wealth Buddha** sits majestically on a dragon inside the pond and he sends prosperity vibes to the dining area and since we spend so much time in this part of the house, we benefit very much from the presence of Dzambhala, especially since I do this practice daily and recite his mantra on a regular basis. The view also extends into the garden which has now matured, so there is a view of some of my prized trees. This signifies my Wood element which generates growth and upwardly radiating energy.

It is so good to have a view of healthy growing plants and trees as you eat. No matter how small your garden may be, when you look at plants, the chi energy generated is growth energy, which radiates upwards and outwards and benefits everyone, but more so when the *Wood element* is important to you.

For me, Wood is my all-important self element and in my chart, my wood is weak, so enhancing and strengthening it with dominant Wood element is very beneficial. The immediate effect of doing this is that it brings many friends into my life – and I can say that I do have a great many truly good friends whom I cherish and love very much… What is great is that Jennifer also has weak Wood as her self element, so like me, Water and Wood elements are excellent for her. Hence the view of water in the pond and a view of the trees in my garden as we eat strengthen us considerably.

The subtle placement and enhancement of any of the five elements that will strengthen your personal chi are always important. It is extremely beneficial to determine these basic things about you if you want to enjoy a smooth journey through life with fewer obstacles than the average guy.

To know which element is favourable and strengthening for you, go to **www.wofs.com**, then click into the Four Pillars calculator. When you fill in your birth and time details it creates *your Four Pillars chart* which you can then analyze using my Eight Characters book on *Paht Chee Analysis*.

Once you know your favourable and unfavourable elements, you will add greatly to your practice of feng shui. This brings the astrological dimension to your practice, which adds to the effectiveness of your personal feng shui.

Mantra On A Conch
Spreading goodness far & wide

The conch shell signifies excellent luck for extending one's good reputation to all the four corners of the earth. In modern days we can equate this with favourable publicity, but this only really tells a small part of this kind of luck. In the old days, the conch shell was always associated with the dissemination of good news, and with the acknowledgement of one's good name in every direction.

When you are able to write meaningful mantras onto the conch shell, the auspicious effect of the mantras also spreads far and wide. I place one of my most precious conch shells in my dining area because this is where we as a family gather together the most. The mantras on the shell were written for us by my very dear friend Charok Lama Rinpoche.

I met him at Kopan in 1997 together with Jennifer when he was five years old, and since then have looked on him like a

Above: **The White Dzambala waterfall sends prosperity vibes into the dining area. White Dzambala who sits on a Dragon is a powerful Tibetan wealth god.**

son and as a member of my family. Charok Lama – we call him Charles – is currently studying at Sera Jay Monastic University for his Geshe degree, a qualification that is equivalent to a Master's degree in Tibetan Buddhist philosophy.

Born in the Year of the Monkey, his astrological energy has great affinity with us, so it is not surprising that he is very close to Jennifer and Chris. Now a teenager, I envisage that one day in the not too distant future, he will surely take his place amongst the great Lamas bringing the precious Dharma to the world.

Sacred Quartz
Empowering crystals with mantras

Charles also wrote mantras, several on natural quartz crystal obelisks, which we display in our dining area. These crystals had been pre-selected by me from a warehouse filled with the most amazing energy, created by the large amount of natural quartz they had there.

That was some years ago when natural quartz was all the rage. They became very trendy decorative items to have in the house and I was not surprised because quartz crystals are such excellent storers of "chi" energy.

Amongst all the treasure that comes from deep in the Earth, perhaps it is natural quartz crystals – in a wide array of colours – that have the most energy accumulation potential.

They bring powerful Earth element energy into any home and are most auspicious and effective when placed in the center of the home. As my dining area is in the center of my house, it makes a great deal of sense for me to place my mantra-enhanced crystal obelisks here.

The mantras are written on the crystals using gold coloured pens and we take great care to select mantras that purify negative karma because it is only when we receive this kind of divine blessings that we can ensure the residents of the house do not fall prey to obstacles and misfortune. In my practice of feng shui, I focus very much on ensuring there are protective vibes surrounding the house always.

Above: **The conch stands for communication. Having a conch in the home creates harmonious communication luck, and when activated by sacred mantras, its effectiveness increases exponentially.**

Facing page: **A Quartz crystal point covered in auspicious mantras by Charok Lama Rinpoche.**

Sitting Orientation
Important to sit right... following Kua directions

While it is important to surround oneself with good fortune chi while eating, it is just as vital to ensure that we are also receiving and replenishing good chi. For this, the sitting direction of anyone as they eat becomes important. Here, it is not so much wanting to sit tapping your *sheng chi* or wealth direction. That is good but even better is to work at ensuring you never sit facing any of your negative directions, more so your "Total Loss" direction.

Use the Kua compass formula of auspicious directions to arrange seating arrangements around the dining table for every member of the family to safeguard their luck every day.

This is what I have done, although I have to confess that I take the easy way out. I simply ensure that every member of my family never sits in a direction that hurts them i.e. their misfortune directions. Naturally, I know the *facing direction of every chair* around the table, so for me, it is easy enough to also direct guests to the right chair. I always select a chair which is good for them!

While following the Eight Mansions method for demarcating lucky and unlucky directions, I also use annual flying star energies to ensure that afflicted directions are avoided. These are known directions for our family as we are great believers of the time dimension of feng shui.

Above: **This Kuan Yin was the very first Kuan Yin I bought when I was based in Hong Kong. Those were the early days of my spiritualism, and when I first met the miraculous Omani Padme Hum mantra. Behind the Kuan Yin statue with two children is another crystal covered with precious mantras than bring blessings to my home.**

Dining With Guests
Glass and Chrome signify Earth & Metal

As we get on in age, we find that we entertain less and less, although every once in a while, we do invite guests for small dinner parties, and while I do go to some trouble to organize a well set up dining table that reflects the modern fine dining experience, for the most part, we tend to be rather casual with friends.

We actually prefer a laid back style (being malaysians) rather than a formal stiff type of dining. I never require my guests to dress up for dinner, so to speak, and everyone is welcome to wear anything they like. This gives me the excuse not to get too high-brow in the laying out the menu or the place settings. When we do invite business associates over lunch – though not very often – we use our other dining room, which is located in the guest house next door.

Yes, I do treat the two houses as being distinctly separate entities – mainly for feng shui reasons – even though getting into the guest house is literally just three steps from the dining area in my old house.

So for entertaining dining, we move over to our guest dining area and here the décor is very different from that of my family dining room. It is furnished in a more contemporary style with glass, chrome and black leather, creating a less traditional look. The décor of this house is something of a concession to my daughter, who prefers the modern decorating style to my more traditional preferences…

We usually serve western or buffet-style food when we entertain, although in truth, no matter what menu we start out with, we usually always end up having some Malaysian favourites. There are three kinds of tables here – two tables with glass tops, one rectangle and one round – and a third table which is also round but made of rosewood and inlaid with mother of pearl. These are the two shapes I like for dining tables.

Overall, although this part of our home appears less furnished than the main house, this is the way we like it. The ambience created is cool and with yin overtones. It is a very public part of the house, so there are a lot less domestic-type paraphernalia or feng shui enhancing decorative objects, although these are not altogether absent. However, the dominating feature here – a giant size photograph of a thousand birds taken by a star photographer student of mine – takes center stage. This picture creates excellent feng shui here as it makes our overseas guests and business associates feel right at home. It is also a great talking point giving me a natural entrée to talking about feng shui…

Patio Dining

We also have very wide spaces outdoors which allow us to dine, mingle and chat in a more casual way – all amidst wonderful plants and with a view of water and active lively fish. We really do love having friends and associates come over and many do, but even more than friends, we really enjoy our family a great deal. The wide outdoors makes it easy for us to plan any kind of dining event.

In the extended patio areas, I try to capture mainly very earthy elements. We also invite in the vital Wood energy, so plants spill over from inside to outdoors and vice versa. This seamless flow of indoor and outdoor chi was done consciously. Living in the tropics, I wanted to capture the magic of the sunlight as well as feel the winds that blow and the rains that fall.

Not everyone appreciates the strong gale winds we get quite often, but I do. Likewise, I also am a fan of the pouring tropical rain which can be very scary, because the waters look so fierce then, especially when you see them in the large monsoon drains that flow outside the house...

> In the garden, a heavy tropical downpour is actually quite beautiful, as every now and again, rainbows form whenever the sun comes out.

Lucky for us, our underground drainage is quite efficient as are our "feng shui" drains, so when the rain gets heavy, these seldom overflow. I make very sure of this actually, since overflowing water is never a good sign in feng shui.

After the rain, the air is clean and cool. The skies are pure blue and the clouds have all been blown away – that is when outdoor dining becomes very pleasurable for the family. This becomes a good opportunity for everyone to imbue the revitalized energy of the great outdoors right in our own garden…

Tortoise Power

We are very lucky to have the upward sloping land behind, as this symbolizes the natural mountain. I have added a couple of feng shui touches ... first, the small but very important tortoise pond where my three terrapins and one black tortoise from India have lived since the early Seventies when the house was built. Tortoises not only bring good fortune, they also guard against premature death and they generate the luck of support. Every house should keep tortoises because they also symbolize protective chi.

Above: **A pair of parrots hang on the wall of our patio area. I picked up this piece on one of my travels and fell in love with it and also with its most auspicious meaning.**

Kitchen Feng Shui

Our kitchen area where food for the household gets prepared has always been located at the back, and from a feng shui perspective, this is always more beneficial than having it too near the front, or worse still, in the center of the house.

Cooking auspicious plays a vital part in any family's good fortune, so the kitchen location is vital to get right. It should never be too small, and it is best when kept neat and uncluttered. Here is where the conflicting but significant elements of Water and Fire come together, so that the cooking area where open fire is used for cooking should never be directly opposite the sink and basin. This creates a confrontational mode causing residents to be also very confrontational with one another.

If you want your family to live in constant harmony, it is important to ensure there are no clashes and destructive element combinations glaringly present inside the kitchen. Reduce both Wood and Metal energy here and never place bright white lights or mirrors inside the cooking area.

The Chinese also frequently warn against having the cooking area on the left side of the house as this creates the misfortune luck of siblings growing apart as they get older. In some cases when the kitchen is on the left side of the house, the second generation will literally be at each other's throats – fighting over the family fortune. This means that the older folk will grow old amidst an atmosphere of hostility.

Thus although this does not affect me much as we have only one child, nevertheless, I am at great pains to ensure the kitchen is more on the right than on the left side; especially the part of the kitchen where we do our open fire cooking. I am very happy with the location of our kitchen, because it is in the Northeast of the property. This is an Earth element corner, which makes it ideal for me. It may not be as beneficial for my husband, but at least it is not in the Northwest.

People whose homes have the kitchen located in the NW are in actual fact causing misfortune to occur to the patriarch of the house. When kitchen is located here, it means there is *fire at heaven's gate* and this causes a very strong and negative effect to afflict not just the father of the house but also generates a bad effect on the the *tien ti ren* trinity that is so vital for good feng shui.

Mountain Star 8

Our kitchen looks out to the upward sloping land at the back, so from the window, what we see is literally a mountain! This has a very powerful impact on us as this mountain basically activates the auspicious *Mountain Star 8* in the Period 8 Flying Star chart of the house. This is very significant as this lucky star is being energized by something natural – the very earth on which the house is built. And because ours is not filled land, the contours around us are real.

When the Mountain Star 8 is so well energized, it brings excellent relationship luck. This reduces and even completely does away with aggravating people and situations. Friendships lead on to good and meaningful ties. And there is little hostility coming in to trouble the residents. Another beenfit is good health and protection against premature death for the residents. Good health luck is as as precious if not more so than wealth luck.

Gold Empowerment

Another thing I did to enhance the back was to literally scatter gold in the mountain out back. This creates the effect of us having a mountain of gold supporting us! It is not necessary to use real gold – simulated gold is just as good! The idea is to empower the real mountain by enhancing its cosmic value. In feng shui, real gold has always played a very important role attracting good fortune.

About twenty feet away from our back fence, there is another house built directly behind us, but at a higher level. This house signifies the symbolic cosmic tortoise, which in turn signifies powerful celestial luck that brings good health, long life AND prosperity as well. The people who lived behind us became extremely wealthy during the Eighties and the Nineties and this was wonderful, because it truly is very excellent feng shui when you are literally supported by someone very wealthy.

Cooking auspicious plays a vital part in any family's good fortune, so it is important to get the kitchen location right.

Facing page: **I love the black wall tiles of my kitchen as these suggest Water energy, although I was careful not to overdo it. This ensures that fire energy does not overwhelm the cooking area.**

PART 5
OUTDOOR LIVING & 11A

We live in the Tropics where there is plenty of sunshine to bring us natural yang chi. My outdoor areas are thus a very important dimension of my home. We have very wide patio areas which benefit from excellent natural light and good breeze flows through our home all day, making it very nice indeed to spend time outdoors. As I am also a keen gardener, this enables me to soak in the beauty of my trees, the blue skies and all my plants. And in the evenings, it is very pleasant to sit outside and gaze at the night skies.

EXPANSION
combining two properties but keeping the feng shui good

Above: **This majestic Kuan Yin made of fine white porcelain sits in splendour facing my dining area.**

Right: **This Kuan Yin sits in what used to be a birdbath in my garden. I have since converted this birdbath into a small pond containing miniature guppies.**

My home was not always as large as it is today. In 2006, I was fortunate enough to purchase the property next to ours. This presented something of a mild dilemma for me because the merging of two properties became something of a feng shui challenge; but it was also fertile ground for me to experiment with some transformational ideas I had on how some of the basic "rules" of formula feng shui can be interpreted to suit modern concepts of contemporary living. Enhancing entrances and creating auspicious luck correctly according to facing directions are all well and good, but I also wanted to create a home that reflected my lifestyle, my need for privacy, for wide open spaces and also to be able to capture the great warm outdoors that I like so much.

I also wanted to simultaneously harness the sunlight which I am crazy about; this is why we choose to live in the tropics; but I also do not like the sun to become excessively harsh. I wanted the light without the glare and for this it was necessary for me to have sufficient land to plant the kind of trees I liked – trees that create shade but not excessively so.

For me, being able to capture the energy of the great outdoors was always at the back of my mind, so I had been trying to purchase the property from the nice lady next door for some time. It had not been easy. She kept resisting my overtures, for a long time even after she moved out… and then one day three years ago she agreed to sell, just like that! It was my good karma ripening of course, because with the addition of the adjacent property, I suddenly would have the garden I was missing ever since our house expansion ate up all my original garden space. Better yet now I could widen my patios and indulge my love for outdoor living…

It has been over two nearly three years since we acquired the property next to ours. Now all I had to do was to seamlessly merge it with the home we have lived in for over 30 years. Our original home had grown steadily in size since we first moved into the neighborhood and as the house grew, so our original garden had dwindled. When my first grandson was born we knew we had to expand our living space, not so much the

interiors but definitely to create more garden space, a place for them to run and romp and soak in nature's sunlight …

I wanted a garden that would be a bright hall harnessing chi for our continued well being and good fortune. Somehow I had to capture the precious energy I knew would settle into the oasis of green I planned to create on the extra land that I had acquired. But how? I knew I had to allow my home to have access to the chi being created. I had to find a way for the chi to flow into my home.

So the first thing I did was to create an opening from my original house to the new garden space now available alongside my home. Would this work? Can I use this side space as my bright hall?

It was in the Northwest, so I interpreted that as auspicious. Apart from adding to my husband's luck, the Northwest is the direction which opens up the Period of 8 for everyone. Why is this? Because if you are familiar with the Flying Star chart, you will know that the chi energy of the chart moves from the center to the Northwest. This also means that the next period number, which in the current situation is 8, is coming to the center from the Northwest. So opening a big door here to welcome in the chi form the Northwest actually means we are making doubly sure that the period of 8's auspicious energy is entering our home.

So I decided my solution of breaking the wall to create an opening to the Northwest to tap into the energy of the new garden would work; and be good feng shui. For me, practising feng shui has always been about common sense and making the best of what we have. I very rarely follow the book so closely as to ignore the realities we are confronted with. So for me, creating an opening into the garden made excellent sense to me, as it in effect transformed that precious new space into a bright hall for my own living space.

Glad to say that now, two years later, the experiment has worked beautifully, for good fortune chi now settles amazingly well in the garden, before making its way into my home through an entrance that is NOT my front door. So now I can tell everyone for certain that the bright hall does not have to be directly in front of your main door. As long as chi from an open space can enter into your home it brings good fortune energy! The key is the doorway or opening – with this in place you then focus your energy on making a really powerful and vibrant bright hall!

Many objects from different countries can be used as symbols of good fortune if they correspond to one of the five elements.

Facing: **A beautiful black Buddha stands in the NW corner of 11A, our new guesthouse.**

Welcoming Lucky Chi

My bright hall brings lucky chi into my home through a side entrance! To entice the chi more effectively I built a wide patio, an outdoor living space that fringes the new opening. An extended roof creates a well shaded verandah that now looks out into a beautiful lawn in the mornings and evenings; and when the lawn transforms into a sea of sunshine in the afternoons that is when maximum yang chi gets created. Believe me it is magical.

The energy that arises is extremely enticing because the warmth of sun is always embracing and never harsh. To create the ambience of peace and tranquility mantras chanted to soft music is played continuously through the day…

In merging the two properties, I also made sure to keep the facing direction of my original house unchanged. I have a SW facing orientation, a direction that is super good for me and I had very painstakingly created it in 2004 when Period 8 came upon us. My pool and fish ponds, my drains and my waterways thus continue channeling good feng shui into the home. The main entrance doors stay the same and there is no need to change anything.

Besides, now the new opening in the Northwest benefits the Patriarch, my husband so on balance the feng shui is very much improved. This new opening into the garden is also diagonal to my SE facing door, the one suited to my husband because he belongs to a different Kua group from me, so the new Door really benefits him hugely as well. but it is also great for me because it faces a West froup direction and I am a West group person.

After building the access for chi to move into my home from the new property, I can then focus all my attention to creating a truly auspicious garden, the all important bright hall where the quality of chi energy created is what determines the quality of our feng shui.

The challenge to me is to make certain that our new "bright hall" the place where good luck chi gathers before entering my home would be bathed with plenty of good energy brought by the sun, the wind and the rain. These are the forces of nature - what makes up the feng shui of any place… Feng and Shui are wind and water; and the sunlight is yang chi that gives meaning to the wind and rain…

Wealth-Bringing Coins

Above: **Acquiring the property next door to our original home allowed us to have the garden I've always felt this house needed. Above is my Kuan Yin pond where my Japanse carp live.**

The new open space was not a pristine plot to start with; the land was uneven and lower than the level of our original house, so it had to be filled with new earth. We had to allow time for the earth to settle. This gave me the excuse to bury some wealth bringing coins into the land. I tied over two thousand coins with red ribbons and buried them all over the garden to symbolically ensure "gold in my garden". Metal energy in

the earth creates the wonderfully auspicious productive cycle of the elements within the earth. Biologically this also adds minerals and metals into the earth making it a lot more fertile! Naturally there are few kinds of land more auspicious than fertile land.It was also necessary to build a labyrinth of underground pipes to facilitate underground water flow. This ensures the garden does not get flooded during our tropical monsoon rainy seasons, a time when the soil can get really heavy and soggy with water. Good drainage is definitely good feng shui as there is nothing

Mountain Star 8 in front SW2 Facing

We did not put a new pond or pool in the garden area in front of the big door into the new house Number 11A because the facing direction of the house was not Southwest 1 as in Number 11 but was instead Southwest 2 so here the lucky mountain star 8 flew to the front part of the house. The Water Star 8 is thus at the back of the house. Placing water in front would thus have resulted in destroying the auspicious mountain star as this would signify "mountain falling into water". Instead, to create *sheng chi* luck based on the *Eight Mansions* formula for the new house, what I did was to build a new carp pond adjacent to the house itself as part of the landscaping of our built up outdoor living area. This benefits guests staying over and visiting us.

Meanwhile, looking at the environmental considerations, I was also very mindful of the multi-level highway that had been built directly in front of the house some years ago. When it was first built, residents had put up a feeble protest as many were fearful the noise level would become unbearable; and that it would spoil the desirability of our residential area. Some residents who felt they would be badly affected sold out and moved away. As a result some choice properties cane onto the market - I guess including the one I successfully bought.

I had a different view. I was thrilled with the direction of the highway - its incoming and outgoing directions were fabulous as they coincided with a little known compass formula on the effect of roads and rivers surrounding one's home. Applying the formula required the careful taking of directions and also making detailed observations of both levels of the road that made up the multi-level highway. Based on my computations, I realized that the new highway, especially the visible upper level road would bring us good fortune. More, the toll gate which collected money from everyone using the highway was near us and it looked like the money was being funneled down to the properties directly below the new highway. I regarded the toll gate collecting money as something auspicious.

But more importantly, from my new garden at 11A, the elevated highway was passing us in a very auspicious angle - all these observations helped me decide to not only stay on in this part of Kuala Lumpur but

Applying any kind of feng shui compass formula requires accurate taking of directions and also making detailed observations of the surrounding "landscape".

more unlucky than clogged up water trapped in the earth. And good drainage also ensures the lawn grows level and springy. as anyone who has gone through this process, it is not easy to ensure this. One has to have lots of patience and in the end it does pay off. Compared to when the grass was first planted on a bare garden, now it is lush and springy and very green and my trees and plants have also matured so that what I now have is a very beautiful and auspicious garden where water flows in a way that brings good fortune to the home.

to expand our property. Property values here have recovered but they have not risen in any spectacular fashion. From our perspective, whether or not our house goes up or down in value is irrelevant as we have no plans to sell or move out. we love our home, and our neighbourhood much too much.

More importantly the elevated highway being so big and high when viewed from our garden actually signifies the mountain and thus activates the lucky Mountain Star 8. This brings excellent health luck and more importantly sends auspicious relationship vibes into our home. It was thus a good decision to make the 11A house into our entertaining area as well as our guest house. The relationship vibes in there are conducive to fostering long lasting and good friendships with people we invite in here.

And so it has proved to be. We have had some truly good times in there with old and new friends… and with students and business associates who come and visit us from different countries.

Sunlit Courtyard

To preserve the feng shui of my old house, I set out to keep the two houses separate so if you take a helicopter view of our home you will see that the two houses are not connected by a common roof and while this causes inconvenience each time it rains, it was vital that the two houses were kept separate this way. If I had connected the two houses, the feng shui of my whole property would have had to be completely redone. By keeping them separate, I made it easier to design the feng shui of both houses.

I decided that an excellent way to keep them separate and yet create a single living space was to create a courtyard between the two abodes with the connecting factor being the flooring material. I used wash pebble finish to create the outdoor flooring as it is easy to maintain and also looks good. it also feels like granite yet is a lot cheaper because it is made up of wash concrete and pebbles imported from the Philippines. Large granite slabs would have cost a great deal more.

A variety of greens, shrubs and flowering plants were used to create a feeling of home… the ambience created is excellent because this is in effect a sunlit courtyard, receiving both the morning sun from the East as well as the evening sun from the West.

much of the sunlight is indirect as tall trees in the garden filter the sunlight at all times of the day. This reduces the ferocity of the afternoon sun and reduces the glare of the evening sun.

Sunlight is a wonderful source of revitalizing energy so that over much of the day we keep our two NW facing sliding doors open. These allow plenty of sunshine chi to enter into the home and more importantly, allowing the free flow of chi is a major factor in preserving the fresh vitality of the home. This also allows the dogs to freely roam around the home. My Cocker Spaniels are super alert watch dogs and they are usually the first to run out to investigate someone at the door. Spaniels have a great sense of smell so they make excellent watch dogs!

Corridor of Buddhas

The sunlit courtyard moves seamlessly into an open space "corridor of Buddhas"- this is where my supper large statue of the Goddess of mercy, Kuan Yin smiles benevolently down at our long finned carp gently swimming in the fish pond.

Different antique and modern Buddha statues stand majestically on both sides of this six feet wide corridor. These specially carved Buddhas are made of hard woods and decorated according to the styles of the village of their origin.

We sit here a lot in the mornings because it is usually cool and shaded. Beautiful white flowering ginger plants create a lovely natural barrier between the corridor and the garden so here is where we read the morning papers, play with our Goldens and also where Jack rides his bicycle and his car…

For me, this is outdoor living at its best in the tropics. And to be able to do this under the benevolent gaze of a variety of Buddhas generates a feeling of calm and contentment. When you constantly see the expressions of the Buddhas, it causes one to also set one's facial expression that way - like creating the habit to smile when staring at the laughing Buddha.

We have a lovely museum quality antique Buddha from India that is standing facing inwards, which is very old, so I surround it with plants to protect it from direct sunlight.

Above: **Different hand mudras mean different things.**

The Buddhas in my garden generate a feeling of calm and contentment. When you constantly see the expressions of Buddhas, it causes you to also set your expression that way - like creating the habit to smile.

Facing page: **Three Mandalay Buddhas with three different mudras.**

We also have two smaller standing monks who are attendants to Buddha in art décor style - also brought in from India. I love them because their coloring are so unusual - serves to remind me that Buddha appears in a thousand different forms and more. Indeed, I have another Buddha piece which is even more 'avant garde' and this sits in smiling splendor just outside my dining area gazing into the goldfish pond. It is encrusted with large colorful crystals and glass inlay... very arty indeed!

Across them I displayed several Buddhas of different sizes imported from the northern Burma/Thai border. These standing Buddhas are done in the Mandalay style, with each of them showing different mudras (hand gestures).

All the Buddhas displayed in my home are regarded as holy objects rather than as decorative items so there are "offerings" placed in front of each of them. This can be flowering plants... offering flowers to holy objects creates the mental attitude conducive to receiving the luck of beauty.

There are also water bowl offerings which have the great benefit of dissolving anger and bad temper situations in the home. It also generates goodwill between employers and maids, and for reducing obstacles that stand in the way of your making progress or attaining success.

We use crystal bowls for this and usually I place either 3 or 7 bowls in front of each Buddha, so every morning my maids wake up at around 5.30 in the morning and spend about two hours changing the water in the bowls. This is a fabulous ritual that brings extremely great merit to them (and to all of us too).

There is a ritual to changing the water in the water bowls each morning because the old water needs to be collected and then used for a productive purpose such as being boilde for making coffee, adding them to my fish pond, my pool or using them to water the plants. these are blessed water and it is a waste to throw them down the drain... then the bowls need to be wiped dry with a clean cloth, and then incense must be used to cleanse them with the words *Om Ah Hum*. This ensures that the water offered is pure and free of contamination of any kind, then

Above: **This Buddha in orange robes stands at the side entrance to the new house number 11A.**

Facing page: **This Buddha is making the prostration mudra.**

only are the bowls filled with water one by one from left to right.

The water must be filled to the top without spilling, and the bowls must be placed in a straight line one grain of rice apart. Following these "rules" is good for the concentration and for focusing the mind. It also adds to the merit of making these water offerings. when there is no water in the bowls they must be inverted so they are closed.

If you leave empty water bowls "open" on any altar it creates the cause for poverty luck. So it is really important, after cleansing the bowls to turn them close until you are ready to fill them with water. Dedicate a jug for offering the water and do not use it for other purposes...

We follow this ritual strictly for all the water bowls placed in front of our Buddhas.. and in all we probably have several hundred bowls to fill each morning. We have been doing this now since 1997 and it has brought amazing good fortune and happiness for my maids. Their children have grown up and gone on to University and one of them has even become a grandmother. She has been with me now for eighteen years so you can see that we do not have maid problems. I am as happy with them as they are with me... and I regard this as a huge blessing indeed.

Their dedication to me is also why mu home is always so spotlessly clean and uncluttered - this is really one of the most basic requirement for enjoying good feng shui. Even this outdoor area is faithfully washed daily! I use low trees and all kinds of plants to create landscaping in this corridor because this is where guests mingle around for cocktails in the early evenings whenever we have friends or family over. In the mornings this is where my husband reads his morning papers...

Prayer Patio

Adjacent to the corridor and the courtyard area is my prayer patio which is part of the old house except now, instead of the garden it used to be, this part of the home has now become a very cozy patio area where I have set up an outdoor altar to do some outdoor prayers, especially when I am doing my weekly incense offering ritual.

The patio here was created after we bought the property next door. I created a low roof here to keep out the direct

Above: **A prayer session in my prayer patio. This was during one of my birthdays when my family and friends arranged for 1000 animals to be saved from slaughter and liberated. It was a wonderful day!**

Many objects from different countries can be used as symbols of good fortune if they correspond to one of the five elements.

Above: **This gorgeous metal Bull with intricate designs on its body was a recent acquisition in the year of the Ox.**

sunlight and because it is wide, the effect is very charming and especially after I was lucky enough to find a beautiful redwood swing that is hand carved with beautiful art décor designs.

The swing is a new acquisition, as is the intricately 'carved' metal bull. These pieces being acquired in the year of the Ox is very auspicious and signifies my wish for the market to "bull" for me!! Wishful thinking of course, but inviting home an Ox in this posture of a bull during the Ox year brings luck to those who have a connection with the Ox. Since both my husband and I have this connection (the Ox is my ally. It is the secret friend of my husband) I was very pleased that we found something like this.

Both the Ox and the swing were made in Pakistan and the reason I bought them was because they looked incredibly well made and beautiful. I highlight this because I want to stress the point that objects that bring good feng shui do not need to be Chinese in origin.

Many objects from different countries are symbols of good fortune if they correspond to one of the five elements. The key to good feng shui is knowing where and how to display these decorative items so that they in effect become cures or enhancers. The other factor to look out for is the energy aura that surrounds objects - especially when we are looking at animals. For this you need to depend on your own inner reactions and use your instincts to guide you.

I trust my own instincts very much, so I rarely bring anything into my home unless I feel an instant affinity. I will also spend time getting to know about the person and the shop selling it to me. This gives me a feel for the energy of the product.

Also in this outdoor patio I have an outstanding life-size **Shakyamuni Buddha** which used to be inside my house but somehow one day I moved it here so Buddha could enjoy a clear view of my bright hall. I may have said this before but because it is so important to keep the energy of the home moving, and to prevent stagnation of any kind, I will say it again.

I move my furniture and my things around every twelve months or so... This ensures that neither dirt nor yin energy formation builds up in any of the corners. indeed if you feel that you are going through a spate of bad luck, you do not need to even know feng shui to change your luck... just move the energy around the major areas of your home and you will find that luck instantly improves. I found a new place for this large sitting Golden Buddha during one of my energy transformation exercises. Do note however that should you move the chi in your house this year it is useful to observe certain guidelines.

Always watch the flow of energy you create as you move your furniture around. Avoid creating blockages. Always use this opportunity to clear whatever clutter may have built up and never forget your directions and elements. In other words, do not make changes that are excessively drastic... and be alert to the results that follow.

Incense Offering

We do not hold pujas or long prayers here. But we use this part of the home - this prayer patio area - to do the once a week incense offering ritual which is so beneficial for ensuring the energy of the home never gets disturbed by negative forces. The incense offering appeases what I call the local landlords and protectors - divine beings who live alongside us in this same space but who inhabit a different realm.

It is important to keep the landlords of our space happy and contented and there is nothing they like more than incense. We Chinese love the aroma of sandalwood so I use this a lot, but I also use Lawado incense which is made from pine leaves collected and dried from the high mountains of the Himalayas.

There is also a special pine tree whose fresh leaves create a fabulous aroma when placed onto burning charcoal. The aroma created reminds me of the high mountains. when I walked up the Himalayas last year I noticed that the villagers there continually burned smoke and incense offerings using pine leaves. When I enquired about it, I was advised that these served to appease the spirit of the mountains thereby keeping the villagers safe from harm.

I do not know the name of the pine tree I use but here is a picture of it. Just cut a few stems fresh from the tree and place them over the hot charcoal. Not only will this create a lovely smell, more importantly it generates beautiful white smoke. Smoke and incense together make a wonderful offering package that is sure to keep the local landlords of your space appeased and happy. It will be even more effective if you can recite the following mantra twenty times

as the smoke rises and the aroma fills your garden and slowly wafts indoors.

Namah Sarva Tathagata Avalokite Om Sambhara Sambhara Hung

In your mind, create the intention that you are offering the smoke and the incense to the all the deities, the Buddhas and bodhisattvas and also to the surrounding devas, local place owners and landlords, and nagas... Ask that the incense can purify the space of all pollutions and degenerate attitudes. Make a strong and heartfelt wish that everything bad is dissolved and all obstacles are pacified.

Incense offerings, done once a week are extremely effective in keeping things moving smoothly for you and your family. I try to do this offering at least once a week - it reminds me of the time when I was young when my mother used to offer smoke incense every Friday. She would go round the house and in e very room let the incense smoke waft in every corner... she told me this would "purify" the home of all the "bad things". But as I grew older and my dad became a more important Government officer, she must have stopped doing it because I do not recall us continuing with this ritual after I became a teenager.

Goldfish Galore

In the same covered outdoor patio, more to the North corner of the home, I also built a six tier waterfall with the water falling into a curved pond and inside this pond I have been keeping varieties of gold fish. Kum yee, the Chinese word for goldfish means gold in abundance so we Chinese are very fond of keeping gold fish.

There are many varieties and for many years I used to keep the Chinese kum yee with the long tail. they reproduced inside the pond to the extent that my population of gold fish just grew and grew... as a result, I gave them away to a friend of mine who had a much larger pond. Believe it or not that year she made a profit of fifteen million dollars on some property investments she bought and sold. Coincidence? Maybe, but it is still something to rejoice!

Today my gold fish pond is filled once more with gold fish, but this time, mine are the fatter variety with the lion head. I have these in several colours and they give me endless hours of joy.

Above: **Regular incense offering rituals ensure the energies of the home do not get hit by negative forces.**

It is important to keep the "landlords" happy and contented, and there is nothing they like better than incense.

If you build a water feature for feng shui reasons, be sure to have a door or window nearby so as to be able to capture and enjoy the good chi that is being created.

Feeding my gold fish and watching them swimming up to me is a joyous morning ritual and I recommend this highly to anyone who wants to benefit from the good feng shui of keeping fish as well as create excellent karmic merit as well. When you feed the fish you are offering food living beings and this expands your store of good karma.

If you keep this variety of goldfish, make sure you also invest in a little contraption that channels oxygen into the water. These little beauties require a lot more oxygen than carps; more importantly, the effect of the oxygen causes bubbles to gurgle up from underwater. This effect creates the most excellent feng shui, because it symbolizes good fortune bubbling up from the Earth. And if your fish pond is in a part of the house that is lucky for you, the good effect gets magnified.

Please make sure that there is a door or at least a window to capture the activated chi that gets created above the pond. Only then can the chi enter into your home.

Number 11A House

This is the number of the second house that makes up our main entertaining area.

It used to be number 13, but the then owner felt the number 13 was unlucky so she changed it to 11A. Actually, that was when I knew inside my heart that someday this property would be mine because my house number is 11 and 11A indicates it is part of 11… which is also my very lucky number.

> According to the Taoists, the day that one is born (you use the Chinese or English calendar according to which one you normally refer to) is considered a lucky number for you especially for gambling and playing simple roulette - things like that.

For instance if you are born on the 28th of any month, then the number 28 is lucky for you; I was born on the 11th of January so 11 is lucky for me… I have put this to the test hundreds of times with happy results.

I thus did not see any reason to revert back to the original number 13 as the number 11A fitted my luck profile perfectly.

To save money, I demolished the front part of the house to make room for a large garden; and kept the back portion. It was basically a renovation job, as I designed around the levels and the foundations of the house, merely hacking away all the walls and resizing the rooms. The space usage was redesigned to allow for a reasonable-sized entertaining area and two guest rooms with attached bathrooms upstairs. On the landing which corresponded to the previous mezzanine floor, I put into place guest toilets.

The feng shui of the house was created to generate harmony and good relationships. I focused on the activating the Mountain Star 8 at the front of the house and opted for a more modern "look" in contrast to my old house. Colours used were thus centered around whites and greys, with heavy use of glass and metal door frames. I have always liked the local white marble so we used these to put in a new floor for the inside.

Upstairs, my guest rooms are quite large and, even if I say so myself, very comfortable. One room is carpeted while the other has a parquet flooring, but both rooms have access to a 6ft wide corridor from where there is a clear view of the elevated highway in the distance. For me, this signifies the essential "mountain' which activates the Mountain Star 8.

The garden is also kept very secluded because I raised the height of the wall so that from the inside, the wall is the standard 5ft high but from the outside, it is a great deal higher. This is because the road outside is lower and continues to slope down. This gives the house an elevated appearance, which is again good for energizing the auspicious mountain star.

It has been over two years now since I started the project of integrating the two houses. Today, my pair of tower trees have soared to the heavens, my three Bodhi trees create a lucky trinity, while my lovely willow is so big now it creates an ambience all its own. It is believed that the willow is a powerful protective tree that keeps out bad spirits and bad people.

Then I simply have to tell you about my three **banana trees**, two of which are fruiting even as I write this. These trees were brought by the birds as I definitely did not plant them and the meaning to us superstitious Chinese is that it means big luck is coming…

The garden has thus matured because even the grass lawn has settled down very well. Our view of the garden is thus manmade and when we look upwards, we always see clear blue skies. Even the elevated road offers a lovely picture, especially in the night, as the

Facing Page: This banana tree in our garden was not planted, but brought by the birds. The meaning to the Chinese is that big luck is coming. Auspicious indeed!

street lamps lighting the highway makes the view very artistic indeed… especially during nights of the full moon and new moon. And when moonlight is available, it turns even the dust in our garden into glittering jewels.

Modern Look

The décor of the new house is more contemporary in terms of looks and ambience. In contrast to the house we live in, here I have refrained from placing too many Buddha images to make it comfortable for those of my friends who are not Buddhist and would thus be more relaxed in a less spiritual looking environment.

Malaysia is a multi-racial country and our people practice a variety of religions. This is one of the intrinsic and hidden strengths of the country and while we are all generally very tolerant and accepting of each other's custom and traditions, still I thought that since we do party here occasionally, and have karaoke evenings as well when some wine and whiskey would be consumed, it would be better left very *samsara*. This means we are all human beings with all our imperfections!

There is a complete absence also of antique or old-style furniture. Instead, what I have used to create a modern ambience are very well-crafted locally made copies of Italian leather sofa sets and perspex coffee tables. I love the feel of good leather, so I do insist that while the sofas may be copied, the leather used is imported, and for this we select the softest and hardiest. This is placed around the television which is always turned on whether or not we come in here during weekdays. My grandsons love playing in this house on a daily basis, so the TV comes in very useful. Here is also where Jack enjoys playdates with his classmates, so the 11A house is really put to good use.

A Thousand Birds
bring good news

Two large photographic prints dominate the hall of 11A; the first one is a beautiful photograph of birds bathing along the shores of a wide river. The birds shown are freshwater birds… and the photograph signifies a million birds ushering in many good fortune opportunities. Traditionally, the Chinese are fond of displaying paintings that depict a hundred birds which apart from opportunities are also wonderful purveyors of auspicious announcements that come from the heavens. Birds bring good news and no home should be without a picture or painting of birds, and the more birds there are in the picture, the luckier these pictures are.

I recall once being introduced to an artist in Singapore whose specialty was to paint a million birds on canvas… these he drew as specks in the distance in a clear blue sky with breathtakingly beautiful detailing of birds close up in the fore ground. And this was the only kind of painting he did.

His works are all specially commissioned by very wealthy clients - mainly from New York - who tend to be very secretive. So he was most reluctant to tell me who they were, but the lady who introduced us was also one of the wealthier ladies of Singapore. In every instance, I was told the birds brought good fortune for those who hung them in pride of place in their living rooms. I cannot afford this artist's paintings as they all start at around a million bucks a piece. Hence I opt for well-taken photographs instead… and the picture of birds in my house was taken by a famous photographer from Eastern Europe.

Hanging in my home, the photograph printed on thick canvas signifies all things glorious that come from the skies… every kind of prosperity brought by a flock of happy birds. This picture benefits my guests more than me, because many go ga ga over the picture, so perhaps that is why many have come back to get their own limited edition print from the photographer.

But I have to say that no matter how beautiful the photograph is, nevertheless, once in three years I do change the pictures or other art pieces that I hang on the walls of my home. So this picture that you see featured in this book will eventually be replaced by another. When I find something better or equally effective to attract feng shui luck, I will likely change it. Doing so keeps the look and the energy young and fresh.

I change the paintings that I hang on the walls of my home because I like energy to be new and vital. This is also the same reason why I usually either throw away my last year's cures or I wrap them up and put them into storage. It is never advisable to use symbols for too long and especially those that have been used as remedies. Having absorbed all the bad vibes, it is usually a good idea to retire them. Besides, fresh and new symbols possess greater strength especially when they are used as cures.

No matter how beautiful an artpiece is, once every three years, I like to change the art and pictures hanging on the walls of my home. Doing so keeps the look & the energy young and fresh.

Facing page: **A photograph of a thousand birds hangs in the hall of my guest house where I entertain.**

Golden Mountain

Above: My home office in 11A where I get a lot of inspiration for my writing. Behind me is a spectacular photograph printed on canvas of a golden mountain.

Facing page: Filming for Astro with the glorious golden mountain as a backdrop.

A second photograph I liked as much as the birds is this one which shows the Golden Mountain. This picture was taken in Canada and the photographer waited patiently for several hours for those few split seconds when the sun shone through clouds to light up the mountain, literally turning it into an ingot of pure gold!

When he first showed me the picture, I was convinced he had somehow expertly photoshopped it on the computer, but on closer examination, I could see that the picture was genuine and completely natural. And since these days all photographs taken are digital, he also showed me the others that were shot alongside this perfect shot.

He asked me if I liked it enough to buy it and of course I said yes. Not only that, I have also made it possible for him to also sell his masterpiece to many of my customers - simply because I am such a great believer in the efficacy and power of sitting with a mountain of gold behind. If you cannot get

the real thing, then a photograph serves just as well. So I placed it on the Northeast wall here in number 11A to signify the mountain of the NE. Needless to say, this activates the prosperity potential and harmonious power of the Northeast. Here the trigram of the NE is *ken*, the mountain.

Many people who have placed this mountain of gold write to tell me of the immediate change in their own confidence level and of course, for me, I am able to tap into this mountain of gold whenever I come over to this work area here to do some writing work. Sitting with the image of a strong mountain behind offers you the precious support that is often so vital for career professionals. It ensures that people in authority listen to you and give support to your ideas and suggestions.

The mountain of gold also symbolizes wealth luck and ensures that should you ever need money, you will always be able to arrange it. Being propped up by such a mountain is incredibly lucky, so it does benefit to invest in a mountain painting or photograph.

If your office is in a high-rise building and you are sitting with a big window behind you, it is a good idea to somehow arrange for a picture or a painting of a mountain to be placed behind you. If you do not there is the danger of your losing the support of influential people.

Roundtable Meetings

My rosewood table with mother of pearl inlay is a very special table which used to be placed in the domestic family dining area… but as my family grows in size I have had to replace it with a larger table. So now I use this auspicious table for meetings with business associates, big clients who come to me for feng shui consultation from all over the world, as well as our World of Feng Shui partners from the United States and Europe.

I like the idea of a wooden round table being used for work type meetings with associates and partners; and for conferencing. My self-element in the paht chee chart is weak Wood, so dark wood is perfect for strengthening me and also creating the good fortune of having important allies.

So many of my meetings with clients, associates, franchise partners, overseas publishers and suppliers are usually held here. Many of them eventually become family friends, so having them over is a treat for me as well. Note that the circular table is excellent for maintaining the equality of everyone seated there. No one is at the head of the table because there is no such placing.

Hence for business meetings this shape table is very diplomatic - and it gives off a good feeling. This is one of three dining tables in 11A so for evening dinner get-togethers, it doubles as a dining table.

This is also the table where we shoot my television New Year clips. So the house 11 A sometimes doubles as a studio of sorts. Many video clips have already been produced here.

Power Lunching

I discovered the power of intimate business dining when I worked for Mr Quek, head of Malaysia's Hong Leong group. Mr Quek rarely ate out in Malaysia… and he had few personal friends. All his socializing was done in his beautifully furnished penthouse which was staffed by an amazingly good cook. Here he would entertain bankers, stockbrokers, investment managers, foreign partners… and politicians, and during the years I worked for him, I was often invited to join them. In the corporate environment of the Eighties period Hong Leong group, getting invited to one of Mr Quek's penthouse lunches was something that was much sought after - and it suggested that the boss thought well of you.

Mr Quek made penthouse dining with him so sought after that partners, bankers and associates alike came to see this as a sign that their relationship with him could be termed "special". It made for excellent networking and was one of the most effective ways of building goodwill with people he wanted to maintain or cultivate ties with.

That was why when I went to Hong Kong to manage Hong Leong's newly-acquired bank, I followed Mr Quek's example and created facilities for having business associates over to our in-house dining room. This was in the bank's penthouse where I created a good ambience for cementing relationships and building a network of allies, which in banking is very important. Unlike other industries, banks usually work closely with each other, sharing credit information as well as giving each other important and timely financial support.

Banks usually reciprocate overtures made to them, as a result of which, many would also invite me to their in-house fine-dining facilities. That was when I learnt how beneficial creating this formal yet intimate setting was in helping to foster friendships and strategic alliances.

In my first year as the bank's CEO, we did really well due mainly to the good support we had from fellow financial institutions. When I floated a special new debt instrument for instance, a 200 million dollar issue of commercial paper, I found little difficulty in getting the whole amount placed in a day… It was excellent indication that our bank was well thought of by other banks.

Since then, I have always believed in the in-house "business lunch", so these days, I also invite business associates home. This creates a relaxed atmosphere and helps to cement relationships. In any case, I prefer eating at home and having people over rather than dining out, mainly because my cook is so good at creating some truly delicious local treats.

From chicken rice to nasi lemak to curry laksa to hokkien mee, I am proud to say we do indeed serve up some great fare. So for lunch time, dining at Lillian's café, haha, we use the rectangular table - a shape that also symbolizes growth. The table is an ideal size… small enough for an intimate atmosphere to get created, yet large enough to seat a perfect 8. It is made of glass, so it signifies Earth element energy keeping us well grounded.

Brainstorming Sessions

Besides using the house for entertaining, we also have some pretty effective brainstorming sessions with our staff from the office here. I feel that because my house is a lucky house, the energy here is conducive to bringing out the best in all of us so I am not surprised that some really great ideas and strategic decisions emerged from these informal sessions.

To capture good feng shui, we usually use the Pa Kua shaped table and we make sure that we each sit facing our respective good direction. From the table, we get a fabulous view of my garden and can even look into the carp pond, so all of us are surrounded by good chi flows.

This is also the South corner of the living area which is conducive to us thinking up ways to make some breakthroughs in marketing, developing new Internet strategies, designing and choosing new products and especially discussing the different findings of our research into what's in store for the coming year.

Personally, I find this to be one of the more significant events of my daily

A circular table is a good way of maintaining the equality of everyone seated at the table.

life. There is nothing I enjoy more than exchanging good creative ideas with my staff led by my daughter, and occasionally with outside designers and suppliers. To have the house space to hold such meetings makes me feel very lucky - and it never fails to drive home to me how privileged I am to still be able to work in such a meaningful way. My house therefore really does double up as a place of work.

Staying Relevant

I feel that because my house is a lucky house, the energy here is conducive to bringing out the best in all of us, so I am not surprised that some really great ideas and strategic decisions emerge from the informal brainstorming sessions I hold with my staff here.

There are many moments these days when I make a renewed pledge to myself to never ever stop working. I love it that I am still relevant to my loved ones and to my staff; and that they think well enough of me to want my ideas, and in fact to respect my opinions. This is both good feng shui and a great blessing - to stay relevant and to know I can choose to always be so.

That is why I tell people I have no intention of ever retiring. I plan to work until the very end… and there is no better way to ensure this than to just keep going. I believe my attitude towards life and work are the best anti-ageing solutions, and for anyone wanting to stay forever young, I do recommend this highly! To be successful at doing this however, it is vital to have a positive attitude. Allow for the fact that those much younger than you have different thought processes. They grew up in a world different from yours, so be broadminded and accepting of their ideas too. Once they know you are accepting of their ideas, they will definitely be accepting of yours.

Once a banker congratulated me that my daughter was so willing to work for me - she said she had seen so many family businesses where the children were often reluctant to join the family business and preferred to do "their own thing". I told her that actually Jennifer did not work for me, but with me. She has all the freedom in the world to do her "own thing" and I respect her views, her prejudices and her hang ups, the same way she accepts all of mine. That's why we work so well together.

More than the body, it is the mind that must stay active. My mum who is 85 years old this year suffers from dementia and Alzheimer's. She is perfectly healthy but her mind is far gone, and looking at her, my heart aches for the vibrant, active woman she once was. The consolation is that she is actually not suffering as she has no memory of anything beyond the past five minutes… but I don't want to lose my mind the way she has lost hers. She is very healthy physically but mentally, it is another story.

So I work at staying relevant. I read. I write. I participate in discussions and debates and make certain that I keep up with what's going on in the world. I also allow myself to have strong opinions, to take sides in controversial issues, because I want my mind to keep working, thinking, analysing…

I do not just follow the financial news, I am also an ardent fan of the gossip magazines, the fashion shows and the movies because tapping into the lighter side of everyone's world does keep the chi flowing smoothly inside my body. This is inner feng shui at its best.

But it is when I am helping my daughter edit our successful magazine **Feng Shui World** that I am constantly challenged. This is what really keeps me and us on the ball. This has to be the most personally beneficial aspect of my work because it forces me to stay very up-to-date about trends, and knowing what's in and what's out! More, to think up good stories and to write them for each new issue, to communicate with my readers - that's what keeps my mind active and alive. Also, being a writer ensures that I place emphasis on being accurate in what I say and write. Believe me, there is nothing more demanding than making sure the written word attributed to one is correct; and that when we have opinions, we must make sure they are defensible.

Writers like me who write non-fiction books need to always stay alert to what gets published under my byline; because once published, words and opinions are hard to take back. The published work is always "carved in stone".

In this I am incredibly lucky in having Jennifer who is a very careful and talented editor. She goes through what I write with a finetooth comb and often corrects my grammar as well! What would I do without her?

Not many people know this, but when she did her A-levels English in the UK out of Benenden School, the teacher told us a year later when we met her at Cambridge, that Jennifer's paper had been marked as the best in the whole of the UK! This is not something we have ever told many people about, but you can imagine just how proud we were of her then. Especially since she left school with straight A's and also won the Maths and Economics prize at school as well.

Computer Literate

Having been professionally active for over 35 years I have seen the work, business and domestic environment of the world change truly drastically over the years and in the past five of these years, change has accelerated even more; to an extent that just keeping up with new developments on every dimension of existence requires an effort. One simply cannot be complacent or ignorant of the way the world is transforming. The issues that concern us these days are different from my early years, and aspirations of people have also been drastically altered by all the new technology that has become available.

The whole world is now connected; increasingly, every mountain top or corner of the earth is reachable and mapped - with just a click I can see my house from space through the magic of GoogleMaps technology, so everyone is now literally visible from cameras in the sky. The whole thing is mind boggling.

All of this is not just due to the invention of the computer and the thousands of software that have been written, but also due to the enormous capacity for literally zillions of information, sound and image bytes that can be stored in cyber space - and all through the invention of fiber optics and other related hardware. When we think of all this and we open our minds to the enormity of the entire galaxy - of worlds beyond our worlds, it is really a very humbling thought.

So in this day and age, no one can stay relevant without being familiar with the computer and the mobile phone. We are in the digital age now and this affects everything we do. Education and communication takes on new perspectives as television and the business of keeping in touch have gone digital. So the homes we live in MUST take cognizance of this new communication and digital revolution taking place before our eyes. It has become

necessary to have several TVs in the house to accommodate different people wanting to watch different channels; but we cannot just stop at TV; we also need computers in key rooms of the home.

Thank goodness I am totally computer literate and without meaning to, I find that I spend at least half the day sitting in front of my various computers... doing research, downloading applications, reading the news, skyping my foreign associates, googling new people and events and checking out Facebook and other websites of which I am a member - and much of this side of my work is done here in 11A, where I have a second office. Good thing I have not started twittering!

You can say that this is my standby internet line (and thus a standby office) - in case the other line in my office in the old house acts up - which it does fairly frequently. Here is also where I play with Adobe Photoshop, absolutely my favourite software. I use it to design new book covers, check out color combinations and design new products.

I find that sitting here with the golden mountain behind me and the garden within view along with my hundred birds picture, I get inspired very easily. This part of the house is quiet and very cool, being well sheltered from the afternoon sun. It is also the Northeast of the house, the sector which in feng shui stands for the rise of wisdom. The NE is also the place of the trigram Ken which means mountain and its number is 8 which makes it resonate then with the chi energy of this period. All very auspicious indeed.

Above: The world is fast changing. Even my 5 year old grandson Jack is familiar with the computer and regularly surfs the Playhouse Disney and Cartoon Network channels on my computer at home.

PART 6
MY GARDEN

Wood represents my self element in the paht chee chart, so I have a natural affinity for plants and trees. Creating a beautiful garden has always been an important part of my living space, and I love having the earth under my bare feet and watching my trees grow.

In feng shui, plants signify growth energy. When they thrive in your garden, you know you have copious amounts of the vital sheng chi. And the garden seamlessly links the two buildings that represent our home, giving us a feeling of space and expansion.

LIVING WITH GREENS
growth luck with plants & trees & flowers

Above: **The sun peeps in through the leaves of my shady Bodhi tree.**

Right: Afternoon sun against my tower trees exude a radiance that brings warmth and brightness chi into my home everyday. I really love the sunshine !

Sunlight Fantastic

Dominating the feng shui of my living space is the ever welcoming yang energy of the tropical sun. Pulsating and bright, sometimes scorching but most times warm and welcoming, I have used it as the perfect medium to transform the "bright hall' we acquired two years ago into a landmark space for my home so that any which way I look out to gaze at it – my garden – the sun's light fantastic creates a thousand reasons for me to feel truly blessed.

If you want to be bathed in good feng shui, make sure the sunshine makes its way into your garden, and into your home.

Even the tiniest porch or patio that welcomes the bright rays of the morning or evening sunshine can be turned into a source of powerful yang chi that never fails to lift the spirits, get you out of a depressed state, bring wellbeing and good health to a sickly body or, best of all, welcome the radiating blessings of the powerful Sun God, Suri.

From the start, I kept an eagle eye on the way the areas of bright sunshine in the garden interacted with those parts of the garden that were shaded. I kept the center of the garden free of plants and trees. Here the sunshine is fantastic and chi settles here magnificently day after day after day, bringing good health, wealth and happiness to us all!

Without the sun, it is impossible to have good feng shui, so if you want to live with good feng shui, make friends with the sun and let it bring powerful rainbows and colourful auras into your life!

Good feng shui is all about attracting, capturing and channeling yang chi into everything we do. It is the yang chi that breathes life and imbues spirit into our every activity.

The bright hall is designed for this chi to accumulate and this has to be created on a daily basis because when the sun sets and night comes, yang chi dissipates, making way for the dark energies of yin chi. So yang chi must be created everyday! It cannot be stored. The good news is that whatever happens, the sun always rises!

My Choice of Tall Trees

Many kinds of trees excite me. I am lucky because everything I like is auspicious, and maybe this is because I love big broad leaves in plants and tinier leaves in trees. I wanted my trees to grow tall and preferably with a single tall trunk that looks like it is soaring into the blue skies beyond.

Above: **Monks conduct a puja in the miniature temple in my garden.**

I do not like trees to have heavy foliage, as **it is important for the sun to filter through the leaves.** This ensures the leaves do not eventually create pockets of yin energy or catch trapped water where mosquitoes breed and bring the danger of illness.

When trees get excessively dense, it is necessary to trim out the interlocking branches. The rule of thumb is to try to reduce of the number of branches criss-crossing within the heart of the tree. Thinning out the trees this way – which has to be done regularly – is what makes trees stay happy and healthy, and as they grow they generate copious amounts of oxygen into the environment.

Not many people know this, but the **growth energy** of trees and plants is what creates the precious oxygen that enables living beings to live on this planet! This is also what brings the pure energy that attracts good fortune! So next time you look at growing trees, say a silent word of thanks.

I also choose trees that do not grow too many leaves. **When a tree is nothing but a mass of leaves, it attracts yin chi.** The mosquitoes love these kinds of trees, as do wandering spirits and hungry ghosts.

Trees are popular sanctuaries for a whole variety of *pretas* and invisible beings that live in a parallel universe from us. Most of them do not cause us harm, but occasionally, when you are unlucky, you can meet a local "preta" or "landlord spirit" that might be harmful. Like the human race, the *preta community* comprises beings of different temperaments. So it is better not to make your compound conducive to attracting them. It is for this reason that yang chi is so important. *Pretas* prefer places that are yin and they avoid places that are yang. This is why they dislike the sunlight.

Having said that, I also take the initiative to keep the spirit landlords of the land who live with us as happy as possible, by observing all the taboos associated with these environmental beings. This means I watch what I say to make sure I do not make the mistake of being verbally offensive to them. It is really important not to be too loose with one's tongue when it comes to things we do not understand…

Once a week, I recite prayers and make incense and smoke offerings dedicated to all the "other beings" that live in the garden with us. This is a ritual that has incredibly wonderful benefits because the spirits who live alongside us are believed to enjoy very much the smell of burning fragrant incense. The best to use for this purpose is to offer the smell of freshly-cut pine leaves. These give off an aroma that is also believed to spiritually cleanse your outdoor areas.

Clump of Bamboo

I have planted a clump of bamboos near the front wall overlooking the road. This is because bamboo must never be planted at the back of the house!

Bamboo signifies longevity and the ability to flow with the wind, so they symbolize going with the flow in the nicest possible way.

Bamboo also attracts many varieties of birds and those that come into my garden do so each morning. These are singing birds and their presence in my garden brings plenty of opportunities. We now have many different varieties of birds nesting in the cleaves of my rooftops and hidden deep inside the bamboo clump. I love having them because birds communicate good tidings from the cosmic protectors of the land. They also direct wealth-making opportunities into the home – so I am never short of chances. Several times each month, someone from some part of the world comes to me with a proposal or other… not that I take them

When trees get overly dense, it is necessary to trim out the interlocking branches. to avoid yin chi formation.

Facing Page: **My clump of bamboo overlooks the road at the front of the garden. Next to it is a bird house to provide shelter for visiting birds although recently I turned it into a garden temple.**

Above: **My two tower trees have grown taller than the house itself and symbolize the "eyes" of my feng shui dragon.**

Facing Page: My "doorbell dogs" Juno & Chester are golden Cocker spaniels who always let me know when someone is at the gate.

all, but it is wonderful that people think of you when they feel they have a good business idea!

Tower Trees

I have two tower trees and these have grown fast and tall signifying a blossoming of aspirations. Now they look like the number 11 which is a very lucky number for me as I was born on the 11th. According to the Taoists if you use the number that is your day of birth, it brings you good fortune. But that is not the only reason; I also wanted a pair of trees growing straight upwards as this symbolizes upward mobility in one's work or career. When trees grow straight and are healthy it signifies good fortune soaring ever upwards. These tower trees add a Zen feel to the garden because they appear so disciplined and determined with nothing distracting them. They make me very conscious of our magnificent view of the skies and the lovely cloud formations above our garden.

It is all in the way our minds work of course, and you can say it is merely my imagination running away with me - but often I see formations of Dragons and Pi Yaos in the skies, sometimes frolicking with a phoenix or two, and other times chasing a golden ball... This conscious awareness of heaven energy merging with our earth and mankind energy is what generates powerful trinity of *tien ti ren*.

So although we live in the valley, we do get lovely views - but my views are of the skies rather than of roof tops or the far horizons… and because Malaysia enjoys such clear blue skies, sometimes this view can be quite awesome.

Doorbell Dogs

Gazing upwards is a good exercise. I look up to the skies in my garden at least once a day, usually in the evenings, as that is when I play with my Goldens - Jumbo and Google. These big dogs of mine are **American Golden Retrievers** and this is why they look like lions really. But they are totally harmless and as friendly as babies. They bring golden chi into the home as they romp freely in my garden during the evening and nocturnal

hours. And although they do not bite, they are great alarm givers. Their bark is loud and clear, so I always know when someone is at the door at nights.

In the daytime, my "doorbell dogs" are my **Cocker Spaniels** and they are nowhere near as friendly as my Goldens. But I love them both to death, both mother and son, Juno and Chester. They too are golden in colour but a deeper, copper gold. They too love romping with me and my grandsons in the garden, making it come alive with their sounds and their barks…

During the nights, the garden is just as lovely and on nights of the full moon, the moonlight glows so bright it bathes the entire garden with quite a magical glow.

We are so lucky – both the sun and moon are clearly visible from where we are and this enables us to inhale in the cosmic chi that brings good health and inner strength. I also find it very easy to energize my personal crystals and mirrors because it is so easy to visualize radiating moonbeams coming downwards. When I want to activate them

with sun energy, I simply place them in the sunlight for three hours… I am very fond of my blue skies and I access their energy on a regular basis. I am not much good at doing exercise and definitely do not know much yoga, but I do know tai chi and used to study martial arts when I was young, so I still remember the movements quite well. This is the exercise I do, usually in the mornings after walking and bathing my dogs, and also at dusk when the sun has gone down… and I have Jumbo and Google cheering me on!

Willows Protect

There are also a couple of varieties of the Australian willow trees that bend so softly with the breezes creating a feeling of easy and relaxed flexibility. I love the willow trees because they remind me of swans, and also because they attract butterflies into the garden. My Willows have grown very big now and it supports several families

of lovely butterflies. Anytime you come and visit me I can show you these winged beauties! Butterflies signify fidelity and domestic happiness and are especially meaningful in the year of the Tiger! So next year hopefully my willow tree butterflies will attract extra good fortune.

The willow tree is also regarded as an excellent safeguard against the evil intentions of others.

In case anyone wants to use black magic against you, the willow tree has the power to deflect it. They are equally effective against any kind of spirit harm and indeed, my superstitious Filipino maids tell me how happy they are that I have such a big willow tree growing in my garden. They inform me that in the Philippines, these trees are always in great demand as they also bring good luck and opportunities.

Mango Tree

My entire garden is surrounded by many varieties of trees, each specially picked for some reason or other, and mostly because I like them. These are grown in a way that creates a bright hall, but also to allow for chi to meander around my garden. So mine is not a manicured garden that is obviously done by an expensive landscape architect. However, I do trim my trees and plants regularly – every week in fact, as it is impossible to do all the trees in one day.

I have some fruit trees to keep the squirrels happy. This includes a very old mango tree which has three strong trunks to symbolize the three of us, me, my husband and Jennifer. This

The feng shui of any property is always reflected in the health of the plants that grow there.

Above: **Blue skies, sunshine and shade combine to bring great vitality, which adds so much to the feng shui ambience of the home.**

Above: **This is one of 3 Bodhi trees in my garden. This one directly faces my Northwest door.**

The Bodhi Trees in my garden were planted to remind me of Buddha Shakyamuni, who achieved enlightenment sitting under just such a tree in Northern India.

Facing page: **I am standing in a very private part of my garden, a secluded area that is planted with different kinds of fruit trees. Next to me is the ciku tree, which is currently fruiting.**

mango tree still gives us tons of juicy sweet mangoes and it fruits all year round. It is as old as the house because we planted it from seed in a pot when we lived in Kenny Hills. We only put the tree into the ground after we moved to our new place. Once, about fifteen years ago, I wanted to build a long swimming pool in front of my house and this required me to chop the tree down. But my husband objected so strenuously I decided to appease him and deferred the building of the pool. In retrospect, I think he was right, because after that, the mango tree seemed to take on a new lease of life… it sent up loads of fresh new shoots and now it looks very lovely next to my giant prayer wheel. In fact, it is now growing in such a way it looks like it is creating shade for the prayer wheel.

Bodhi Trinity

There are three Bodhi trees in my garden. These create a holy triangle and remind me of my the time I travelled to this most holy of cities in India to keep a date with Lama Zopa Rinpoche, this high lama who had contacted me to invite there and I had gone,

compelled by an inner force I could not resist even though at that time I had little interest in things spiritual. That was my first time in that city, and also in India and it happened in 1997. That was a magical year and since then I have become so enamored of the Buddhas I have filled my home with them.

The three Bodhi trees in my garden are to remind me of Shakyamuni Buddha's Enlightenment, achieved while sitting under just such a tree in Bodhgaya in Northern India. One tree thus has been planted just outside the doorway so that from inside the house I can see it. Under this tree, I have placed a lovely wooden carved image of Buddha sitting in meditation under the Bodhi tree even as five nagas rise in an attempt to distract the Buddha.

This is what prompted Shakyamuni to extend his right hand to touch the Earth, asking the Earth Goddess to attest to Buddha's mountains of merit and thus bear witness to the attainment of enlightenment. I think this is so beautiful a scenario to re enact and so it takes pride of place in full view of the house so anyone who comes can see it and be inspired. The bodhi tree here is grows very fast. It looks like an umbrella shading Buddha from the direct sunlight. Because

of its connection to the Buddha tale of enlightenment, many regard the bodhi tree as sacred so I like many Buddhists feel a special connection with this tree.

A second Bodhi tree shelters the prayer wheel, while a third is placed directly in front of the elevated highway in the distance. I want this third tree to eventually grow so tall as to partly block off the highway…

Now what it does is provide some shade to this part of the garden wall enabling the shrubs that need to be shaded from the sun, to grow better. I am always mindful of the health of my plants as I believe they create the chi energy for everyone living her to enjoy good health.

Crystals in the Trees

One of my favourite rituals to enhance the feng shui of my indoors and garden spaces is to hang small faceted crystal balls on the branches of trees and also on the grills on my windows. The idea is to place them so strategically as to catch the sunlight directly. This has the effect of creating rainbow light which radiates outwards.

It is really effective when the sun is shining brightly and then, every now and again one of the crystals will send out radiating light - that is when the garden and also the living areas come alive. This is what makes the house so special because the crystal rainbow lights is what manifests the invisible cosmic forces coming together in an auspicious display.

The radiating brightness is also very spiritual as it infuses the whole of my outdoor patio area with fire power. This brings recognition of my work and my books and creates marvelous good feng shui that benefits not just me but all of us.

Jacaranda Lilac

This is a very lightweight tree with little feng shui significance but for me and my husband it brings back fond memories of our early days in this house. That was when we had to make every dollar count as we were both employees he with Tenaga, the Electricity utility company and me with MIDA, the Govt Investment promotion body overseeing direct foreign investments into Malaysia; so our income each month was fixed and it always seemed woefully inadequate but even then we loved dogs and

we loved trees so these were the luxuries we spent our money on.

Our Jacaranda tree always bloomed profusely and it littered our driveway with lilac flowers each time March or April came round… later, we lost that tree and it took a very long time to find a replacement. The one that grows in our home now is still a young tree, but already it has started to bloom. We see this as a very good sign. Looking at the Jacaranda makes me feel mellow. It reminds me of the old times. So it has a grounding effect on me…

My Greens & my Flowers

We all know of course that Mother Nature is anything but static especially in the tropics. Here in Malaysia, the sun shines all year round and there is plenty of rain as well. So everything grows really well and really fast here. There is a need for constant pruning and daily raking of leaves. The rule about watching out to ensure space does not get cluttered applies equally to the garden around the home so I make sure we clean our garden of dead leaves on a daily basis.

I also have many beautiful varieties of ornamental leaves and shrubs that grow in great and happy profusion. I have always maintained that the feng shui of any property is always reflected in the health of the plants that grow there. When the plants look happy and healthy, you can be sure the feng shui of the space is likewise in robust condition. When plants look sickly, that is when you know something is wrong with the energy.

In fact before you buy any property it is not a bad idea to look out for just such signs to at least have an idea of the kind of energy that pervades the space. Sometimes even the weeds cannot grow despite there being nothing wrong with the soil and then it's a good idea to think twice.

One of the key components of good feng shui is of course the presence of sunlight. While it is not good to have too much sun - excessive sunlight burns! - sunlight should never be missing. when the sun cannot penetrate through into the property, and especially the garden because the trees are overgrown then it is likely that yin spirit formation has already taken place.

Different plants have different appetites when it comes to sunlight.

Some of my plants prefer the afternoon sun; some appreciate just a little bit of

Above: It is extremely good feng shui to have at least one lotus plant in the house, as this represents energy in its purest form. I have several and this one sends up white blooms.

Trees in your garden can exude protective energies, especially when you nurture and care for them. You have to trim them, fertilize them and treat them as part of your family.

Facing page: These three trunks of my 35 year old mango tree creates wonderful protective energy for the whole house. My husband is especially fond of this tree which we planted from seed in a pot before moving to this house.

Above: **The precious pink lotus flower symbolizes all that is pure and beautiful in human nature. This particular plant blooms quite regularly and each time the flower is so perfect it reaffirms its exquisite purity. .**

sun and a lot of shade and some prefer to be out of direct sunlight altogether. But my experience has been that almost every growing thing needs and loves the sun. In fact nothing survives without it. Grass that is in the shade a hundred percent of the time simply dies from lack of yang chi and so do plants whose soil have no chance to dry out because they are never in the sun.

The sun is the source of life-bringing good fortune auras day after day!

My plants do exceedingly well. But that is because I am ever conscious of the sun.

I watch it closely as it travels along its path during the course of a day, focusing intently on where the light is in the mornings, how it changes through the day and how it affects different parts of my garden and outdoor corridors and patios, at distinct times of the day.

My flowering plants cannot seem to get enough of the sun, so I make good use of the golden rays wherever and whenever they shine. I go to great pains to ensure that my flowering plants are given the sunniest spots. So my home is always a profusion of blooms and because tropical flowers come in such vibrant colours I love it each time my collection of flowering plants send out flowers.

Flowers Symbolic

If you want success to blossom and bloom for you all the time, then live with flowers. They symbolize the arrival of many kinds of good fortune like few things can. Flowers lift the spirits because they touch the soul with the perfection of their Mandala.
Everyone is charmed by the vibrancy of their elemental significance, hence for centuries and amongst all cultures, flowers are loved because they manifest so many kinds of good fortune happenings.

This is why flowers are always used to celebrate happy occasions. All the double happiness events of our lives are never complete without the presence of flowers, from the celebration of birthdays to the remembrance of loved and dear ones.

Marriage festivities are incomplete without flowers and the birth of children are always commemorated with flowers, as are occasions of attainment such as graduation galas, when we rejoice at getting a new job, observe the happiness of getting a promotion, or when we honour a loved one or make merry at a special occasion such as an anniversary or special dedicated day...

Flowers are a great way to dress up the interiors of any home OR the appearance of any garden. They breathe life and colour into living spaces dominated by yin-styled interiors. Bricks and mortar, glass and chrome can be forbidding and uninspiring but their energies are easily transformed. It all comes to life, their clean lines getting accentuated and softened, made more enticing by the mere presence of flowers.

My home is never without flowers. They make their presence felt in every corner and every room, and over the years, I must have spent a small fortune buying fresh flowers. They look lovely but can easily become bad feng shui when they wilt and fade by the end of the day. Even hardy orchids lose their luster by the second or third day. We do not need anyone to tell us that wilting flowers simply cannot be good feng shui! The worst is the water in which they stand, which gets progressively yin, stale, dirty, smelly. Vase water which should be clear and clean often exudes an odor that emanates bad chi when flowers start to fade. What was good feng shui can thus easily become harmful feng shui very fast unless the water gets changed daily...OR you can use artificial man made blooms especially those that are well made.

Above: **Bright red peonies are excellent when placed near an entrance into the home. The decorative leaves here are known as "elephants ears" although they look nothing like that !**

Crimson Delights

In feng shui, the colour Red signifies the Fire element that can effectively burn all your misfortunes, your bad luck and all the disharmony of the space.

Red is the ultimate good luck colour, so it is always a great idea to have some red flowers in your garden. They signify success and power, recognition and fame. Red is also the colour of the South so placing red flowers in that corner will be excellent. But they also look good everywhere.

In my garden, inside my patio, I have a bunch of red peonies. Here the artificial blooms blend in stunningly with the natural leafy plants and I have noticed that when I clip these peonies they seem to make the green plants look even more lush. Amazing what a little creativity can do to make plants look even better than they already are. Together they create a splash of vermillion that generates extremely good feng shui energy. I also have a bougainvillea plant with red blooms which also plays host to the same manmade peonies and these too blend in so well with the real blooms.

No matter how small your garden, it is very beneficial to take advantage of weather conditions to create a friendly forest-like ambience.

This part of my garden exudes nurturing energy that is conducive to contemplation.

Main picture: **I call this my meditation walkway. You can see that on a sunny day, it is a beautiful mix of yin and yang shade and sunshine. At nights, through clever lighting, this part of the garden is turned into a very special place for walking meditation.**

Gardens can be made into very special places within any home because here is where the universal cosmic chi settles and accumulates naturally. This is also where we can harness the forces of nature, the sun and the rain, the breezes and the winds to produce a store of lucky energy that is never ending, always enduring... this is what I have tried to achieve in this corner of my garden.

Main picture: At night, after a light shower the leaves glow with a special radiance. It really is quite magical then.

Lavender Glories

Shades of purple that reflect the varying intensities of the colour lavender are extremely lucky in Chinese feng shui reckoning. In fact the colour purple signifies money and when matched with silver the symbolism becomes quite awesome. Purple is always used to describe great good fortune that ripens so well that it is not mere good luck but purple good luck! Another way of expressing it is that luck is so red it becomes purple!

To Westerners, the lavender plant always signifies calm. They associate the lavender aroma with feelings of relaxation and so it is. Here we can view lavender flowers as

Above: It is really a great challenge to make these imported begonias bloom in the tropics, but I have noticed that when the temperature falls during the rainy season, my begonias oblige me by sending beautiful blooms like this one. I am especially fond of this lavender colour.

the manifestation of the glory that comes with achievements and attainments. When lavender flowers are sent in bouquets they bring this wish for success. When placed near your entrances, purple or lavender flowers signify great good fortune associated with prosperity and attainments.

You can create a profusion of flowering lavender plants flanking your entrance doorway into the home. There is nothing luckier that welcoming the chi this way. You can place them in any way you wish, but they must create an ambiance of abundance if they are to bring you good fortune.

You can also create a sense of depth using blooms of different colour tones, especially done in lavender as these create a sensation of relaxed confidence.

Orchid Tropical

When you live in the Tropics like I do, there is simply no excuse for not taking advantage of the way Orchids just flourish. Our humid weather is incredibly well suited to these royal plants of the Equatorial jungle although it has been well over a hundred years since modern Botanists have discovered these long lasting and velvety beauties. Orchids flower through the year so they symbolize the flowering of success luck all year round.

The Orchid is often regarded as the king of flowers in feng shui probably because there are five petals to the Orchids and the number 5 has great significance.

Not only is 5 the original center number of the Lo Shu, it also signifies the five elements that encompass the whole Universe. In feng shui theory, everything emanates from the five elements and the Orchid symbolizes the presence of all five elements. Five petal flowers are also regarded as very precious by Buddhists as these signify the five element cosmic Buddhas.

Many varieties of specially cross-pollinated Vandas, Phillinopsis, Dendrobiums, Cympediums and others have been created in the greenhouses of Orchid Enthusiasts here and elshere in Asia, so that Orchids now come in a profusion of colours, shades, sizes and even the way the petals interlace with each other.

These days real orchids have become so perfect they look almost fake and of all the flowers that are being "made" by the deft fingers of the maidens of the Chinese flower factories.

Orchids look the most authentic. When I clip them to my real orchid plants they not only instantly makes my collection come alive, wonder of wonders, they also somehow cause my real orchids to bloom more frequently as well! If this is not good feng shui! In any case, they cause my real orchids to look really great near my prayer wheel and they make beautiful offerings to this powerful sacred holy object.

Above: **These orchids are manmade but look so real when I attach them to my real orchids. They even make my real orchids flower better and more frequently!**

Green Dragon

It is auspicious when you invite the Dragon into the home as this regarded as the most auspicious creature in feng shui. The Dragon brings rain and sustenance to human beings and to the Chinese the water dragon brings wealth and prosperity. The Green dragon brings success and all the goodies that come with success. And this is the dragon of feng shui. If you can somehow simulate the presence of the green dragon in your house, it is definitely very prosperous.

I have already shared my personal connection with the dragon with you in the earlier pages of this book so you already that I have many dragon images and statues inside my home. But I also have "green dragon" which I created from a variety of

green plants along my left side of my hose. This corresponds to the SE side of the house so here plants and greens strengthen the presence of Wood element here.

My Green Dragon has been in existence here ever since we built this house.

The Dragon of the old days used to be more sparse and lean. In the early years, I was less passionate about feng shui and did not pay sufficient attention to it... but later, several years after I returned from Hong Kong, I started creating the Dragon's presence with great earnest. I chose the plants more carefully so that the head, the limbs and claws as well as the body and tail of the Dragon were carefully differentiated.

Above: **This is the Green Dragon. It goes all the way from the front to the back of the house. It comprises of a variety of tropical green shrubs.**

As soon as the Dragon emerged from the plants this way, i.e. symbolically, our fortunes took a steep increase. That was when the books became very popular and our lives became hectic with international travel.

For many years after, my books became bestsellers around the world, and I was invited by many international organizations, corporations and clubs to speak at events and gatherings... Incredibly, I was always paid for these speaking engagements, and they also paid for my travel and hotel expenses. And we were always put up in five star hotels everywhere we went.

Those days were amazing... at that time, Jennifer was studying for her Economics degree at Cambridge so my husband and I did a lot of travelling. The countries we visited in connection with feng shui included Russia, China, Australia, USA, Canada and many cities in Europe...

I also did a ton of Radio, television and press interviews as part of my agreement to promote my books. These were arranged by my foreign publishers, **Element Books** which now belongs to **Harper Collins**; **Random House**, **Cico Books** and also **Barnes and Noble** and **Borders**, the last two being bookshop chain stores in the United States, and they had their own publishing imprints; so I also did some books for them.

I always suspected my success was brought about by the presence of Dragon images in my home with the most powerful enhancer being the Dragon created by my plants.

Those of you born in the years of the Rooster, the Snake, the Monkey and the Rat especially will benefit from the kind of Dragon I have created in my garden. This is the way I have done it and have benefitted from it all my life. You can too.

Private Park

I think of my garden as my private park; a sanctuary where my grandchildren can play safely and enjoy the great outdoors. The

whole garden is in fact cleverly hidden from view so no one can actually see the garden. This is because of the way it has been built but also because it is surrounded by tall trees. Homes that look ordinary and small outside but are really large and spacious with hidden gardens inside are more auspicious than homes that look big on the outside but feel small to live in.

My garden is a sea of green... the colour green is both soothing and relaxing and a lawn of green grass does wonders for the soul. It took three years to get the lawn perfect; that's how long it takes for the grass to mature and settle in. One sign that your grass is doing well is when you start to see "worm mounds" in the mornings and we had plenty of that. And then the birds came and ate their way through my garden... it will take at least a whole season for the worms to return.

This is where my friends and I hold special "liberation of animals" pujas to celebrate birthdays. We go to the market to purchase pigeons that are meant to be sold and eaten... and then after reciting powerful mantras, we release these pigeons, in effect liberating them. Even if they do not survive, the prayers benefit them hugely.

Above: **This bush represents the Dragon's claws. It is part of my Green Dragon in the East sector of the house.**

Below: **A yellow hibiscus in my garden.**

Overleaf: **Animal liberation in my garden.**

Money Shrubs

A plant I am very fond of, which I think of as being a prosperity attracting plant is this robust growing shrub. It has round leaves that are thick and waxy and when these leaves turn yellow, that is when "money" drops from it. This plant is believed to attract a steady flow of income into the home, not necessarily a big flow but a steady one. I place this plant in the eastern flower bed that signifies my Green Dragon, at the front facing the main gate. Another plant that serves the same purpose of attracting wealth are plants that have thick, succulent leaves that remind me of jade, the precious stone the Chinese equate with wealth and which I am so mad about.

White Ginger Flowers

This lovely plant sends out the most beautiful white flowers that make excellent offerings to the Goddess of Mercy statue in my home. Two stalks of this plant were first given to me by my nephew and these have reproduced into several clumps in my garden. And wherever I grow them they send up long slender stalks of white flowers. The key to making them flower is to feed them enough sunlight but not too much, and to trim down the older stalks.

Garden Walkways

It is great to have wide walkways around your garden. Those that lead to any of large opening or door into the home should definitely be wide and are better curved rather than straight and narrow. They do not need to meander but it is more auspicious if they curve gracefully rather than turn sharply. The wider the walk, the more welcoming and when it is slightly curved, it allows chi to slow down making the pathway more auspicious. The longer the walkway, the more harmful it is if straight as this causes energy to move too fast.

Soften walkways. If you want your walkways – corridors and patios alike – to achieve an ambiance of relaxed abundance always make an effort to soften the effect of stones, tiles, chrome or glass by creating pockets of green and flowers. The hardness concrete always benefits from the presence of plants and flowers.

Top: **Glorious shocking pink hibiscuses add beautiful colour all round my garden. They flower daily, and the flowers last only for a day, reminding me of the impermanence of life.**

Above: **My money plant, whose leaves remind me of pieces of jade, a gemstones regarded by the Chinese as symbolic of refined wealth.**

Facing Page: **My white ginger flowers.**

Sometimes you can also place - like I do - celestial and not-so-celestial protectors. I am very fond of elephants so you will these all over my gardens and walkways. The presence of these "creatures" whether real or simply manmade creates the yang chi of living beings so here on these pages I show you all the creatures that live in my garden.

A brass bull placed on a small table in my outdoor patio corresponds to the Northwest sector of my home here to bring amazing good luck to the patriarch, my husband. Wan Jin dabbles in the stock market to keep himself occupied. He has been doing this ever since he retired some eighteen years ago so I make sure he does not "lose" money. The Ox is his ally and secret friend so getting an Ox to make the market bull for him is sure to bring him some good speculative luck.

A pair of deer placed at the doorway of the sliding door that looks out into the bright hall symbolizes longevity. The deer is also believed to "open up the mountain" which in feng shui terms means bringing plenty of good things. So having this beautiful pair here with well-developed horns suggests not only abundance, but also protection.

I also have a pair of giraffe... this lovely couple has no special significance and I invited them into the home simply because I thought they were so beautiful. They look extremely happy placed near my carp pond.

Then I have a pair of camels. These have been with me for several years now. They were a gift from students of mine from Uzbekistan, and she handcarried them all the way from her home. These are camels that ply the Tashkent desert, and of course, camels signify the ability to survive under the harshest of conditions. they are creatures of the desert and they can go without water for days… so I have placed my camels near to my prayer wheel signifying the arrival to this holy place after a long journey.

I also have a pair of Phoenixes that flank the doorway of my Southwest facing front door; and many pairs of elephants both with tusks up as well as down. I have elephants that come from India, China and Thailand; I have them made of wood, brass, jade and porcelain and I see them as sacred friends of mine that bring plenty of good fortune and this is because almost all of them were gifts from good friends.

In India and Thailand the elephants are regarded as sacred animals and they too believe that having them in your home brings prosperity, safety and abundance.

When you plant fruit trees, each time they bear fruit, it signifies the manifestation of some dearly held wish. And because of this, growing fruit trees is very good feng shui. The only problem is that fruit trees do attract squirrels and birds, which can be quite an inconvenience.

Main picture: **I am very proud of this Red Jambu tree which is planted in a pot and which gives me fruits twice a year.**

We live in the valley where the breezes that blow are extremely gentle. Our view is of blue skies and on a clear day, it is really fun trying to find Dragons and Pi Yaos in the cloud formations.

Sometimes there are so many Dragons that I know something wonderful is coming...

Main picture: **Picture taken on a bright and sunny day shows my beautiful trees silhouetted against the bright blue sky.**

PART 7

HIGH LAMAS COME VISITING

I strongly believe that the excellent energy that pervades my home is a result of the zillions of blessings brought by Lama Zopa Rinpoche and the other high lamas who have stayed in my home. Their mere presence is enough to attract powerful cosmic forces that create an aura of love, compassion and kindness feelings for my home, helping me to overcome obstacles to my Dharma practice and generating the bodhicitta sentiment so strongly here.

In the past 12 years, Rinpoche has visited eight times, while my dearest Charok Lama Rinpoche, with whom I have such a great affinity, has spent many year-end vacations with us.

We have hosted the incomparable Kyabje Choden Rinpoche and also Dagri Rinpoche and the wonderful Khenrinpoche Lama Lhundrup, the Abbot of Kopan Monastery in Nepal; and also the adorable reincarnation of Geshe Lama Konchog, Phuntsok Rinpoche who is two years older than Jack... and to cap it all, we have had the excellent good fortune to welcome sweet Khadrola into our home.

Then in December 2009 the young reincarnation of HE Ling Rinpoche, senior tutor to HH Dalai Lama visited us. Picture here shows Josh and Jennifer receiving blessings.

SPIRITUAL AWAKENING
meeting the high lama

Above: With Lama Zopa Rinpoche

That fateful day in February 1997 when I met Lama Zopa Rinpoche was the ripening of a past life karmic merit that would awaken a deep spirituality within me and change my life forever...

Far right: Lama Zopa Rinpoche leading a prayer session in my home. Rinpoche came many times to visit with us, each time passing on precious gems of profound wisdom on how to tame our minds by understanding its true nature. To my family, Lama Zopa is a living Buddha and our total devotion to him has brought us incredible blessings which manifest in so many ways, both material and spiritual. My success in feng shui is a direct result of Rinpoche's blessings.

It began in 1997 the year my life changed. That was when I received a fax from **Lama Zopa Rinpoche** - at that time I had no idea who he was - who invited me to meet with him in India. He asked me if I would like to take a look at the land where he planned to build a big statue of **Maitreya Buddha**. He said he had read my feng shui book and that he thought it would be beneficial for me to see whether I could help them with the feng shui of the site earmarked for the project.

With every intention of refusing his kind invitation because I did not feel adequate to such a big challenge, I nevertheless found myself flying to Delhi, being met by a tall handsome Dutch monk called **Ven. Marcel**, and allowing him to bring me to **Bodhgaya** to meet the lama. We took a domestic flight to **Patna**, and from there motored to Bodhgaya - a four hours drive across rural India, on the way passing dried out rivers and very poor villages. When we arrived, I was told the lama had not yet arrived, but very comfortable quarters had been arranged for me...

Past life karma

The fateful day in February of 1997 when I met Lama Zopa for the first time was the ripening of a past life karmic merit that was to awaken a deep spirituality within me and see a flowering of inner change that would transform my view of life and living forever...

I had just embarked on my life as a writer and feng shui expert. My locally published feng shui books had been enjoying excellent success in Malaysia and Singapore although I had not yet made it big overseas. But a British Publisher, **Element Books** was about to release my first internationally published book called *The Complete Illustrated Guide to Feng Shui*. I did not know it then but years later I was to come to realize that my meeting with Lama Zopa in Bodhgaya was to create so many blessings in my life that, it was to bring so much success to my work in feng shui - as a writer, speaker, advocate and consultant.

Rinpoche himself was incredibly interested in my feng shui work and in the initial years of our relationship, Rinpoche spent a great deal of time talking about feng shui with me, and asking a great many questions. He expressed a wish to see my house and that gave me the courage to invite him to come and visit.

By then, I had come to realize who he was, that he was a very, very high lama of the Tibetan Buddhist Tradition and that he was the **Spiritual Director** (i.e. the boss) of a large and influential Buddhist organization based in the United States called the **FPMT**. The full name is something of a mouthful i.e. the **Foundation for the Preservation of the Mahayana Tradition**.

This FPMT had over a 150 Buddhist Meditation Centers in five continents so as its head Lama Zopa Rinpoche had hundreds of thousands of disciples all around the world!

It was heady stuff meeting him. I did not even know how to address him, but they told me to address him as **Rinpoche**, which means "Precious". He is regarded as the Guru, the Lama by his disciples so they call him Rinpoche, a widely accepted term of devotion... so I called him Rinpoche too. From the start I was very taken with Rinpoche, and I believe, so was he with me.

We established very quickly that we had lived a past life, perhaps many past lives together. We had so many incredible and mysterious conversations, and I found myself telling Rinpoche so many things about the details of caves and journeys, of us flying in the skies and me falling down mountain sides and shivering in the cold... things that surprised me. I thought I was being quite absurd, but Rinpoche made no comment, only smiling and raising his eyebrows and allowing me to ramble on and on. Then he would ask me how I knew the size of the cave and the height of the door...

things like that, and that was when I shook my head in amazement because honestly, as I told Rinpoche, I had no idea how I knew…

But I was very keen to invite him to come and be my guest, to come and meet my family. Unsure of the protocol I turned to Ven. Roger who assured me that all I needed to do was ask.

The first time Rinpoche came to our home was later in the same year 1997. That was when he visited Kuala Lumpur to lead a retreat and give teachings organized by the FPMT center in Malaysia. Surprising myself, I successfully did the retreat. Then later I even took the Chenrezig (Compassionate Buddha) initiation from Rinpoche, in effect taking him on as my guru, my lama.

The Tibetan Buddhist Tradition takes the establishment of Guru disciple relationship very seriously. For me, I was simply overjoyed, because by then, in the short two months following my meeting with him in Bodhgaya in India, Rinpoche had come to mean very much to me… so much that when the FPMT gave me a list of "guidelines" on how to host Lama Zopa, I was more than happy to adhere to their 'rules"…

At some unconscious level within me, I just knew that Rinpoche visiting and staying over at my house would **bring incredible blessings to my home, my family and my life.** So when he accepted my invitation and told me he would be coming to stay for a few days after his teaching schedule at the KL center, I was literally over the moon!

Top: **Rinpoche surprised me on my birthday by visiting my Extravaganza talk in the year 2003. It was the best birthday present ever.**

Above: **Driving with Rinpoche across America on the way to his house in Seattle, in Washington State. That trip Rinpoche taught me how to overcome impatience by keeping me waiting for him in Salt Lake city for two days. Note Rinpoche's magical mudra above my head created with little finger and forefinger.**

Before meeting Rinpoche my knowledge of Tibetan high lamas had been confined to a book I had read when I was a teenager called "The Third Eye", so the only thing in my head then was that high lamas were supposed to be able to do astral travelling, leave their physical bodies and fly wherever they wished to go… of course I did not believe that was possible.

Since that year of course, I have learnt a great deal about Mahayana Buddhism. In Rinpoche, I had the best teacher possible and in the past twelve years since meeting Rinpoche, he has opened my eyes so much. I have been very inspired by his incredible purity and although it has sometimes been very hard to practice all that Rinpoche teaches, nevertheless, because Rinpoche is so incredibly skillful, I find myself today a much changed person.

Hosting Lama Zopa

That first time hosting Rinpoche in my house was very stressful. Following the guidelines was harder than I thought. Everything to be used for and by the high lama has to be new, unused and untainted by anyone else. So I had to quickly get new bed sheets, towels, blankets, soaps, plates, cups, glasses, toiletries, cutlery, pillows and so forth... and because Rinpoche had diabetes, he had a special diet which had to be strictly followed. Rinpoche was a vegetarian, so out of respect, we usually also become vegetarians whenever Rinpoche visits.

Then there is the matter of Rinpoche's routine... from the early hours of the morning, Rinpoche does practices and these require hours of prayers and although we may serve lunch at noon, there are days when Rinpoche does not finish his prayers until way past midday.

Once we waited until six to eat lunch because there was an emergency requiring Rinpoche to do a special puja for a disciple who was dying. Another time, we did not get to eat lunch until midnight!

So there is no timetable and over time, I learn to get used to Rinpoche's ad hoc schedules. Another thing is that Rinpoche usually takes about an hour to bless the food each time we sit down to dine. Once my husband sat down to lunch with Rinpoche, it was about one thirty in the afternoon, but by the time they ate, it was 3 pm. Rinpoche had taken so long to bless the food that everything had gone cold. These days Rinpoche, having successfully taught us all patience, takes much less time to bless the food.

Rinpoche teaches in incredibly skillful ways. He is very very patient, rarely direct, and I have discovered that every single word he utters has a meaning and a reason. He taught me so much about holy objects, explaining their benefits to me in great detail. Rinpoche said many times, over and over again, how important it was for us to purify our negative karma and create merit! And because he has so much understanding of our impatient busy lifestyles, he extracted the easiest ways for us to do so, translating precious texts from the sutras.

Top: **Rinpoche gave my family and me teachings when he visited us in April 2005.**
Above: **Rinpoche carrying Jack when he was 10 months old. Lucky Jack !**

Blessing Power
Of The Buddhas

Creating karmic merit does not have to
be difficult. Indeed, Rinpoche's style makes
it so easy. Live a good life never harming
people, he tells me from the start. Live your
life always benefitting others; be mindful of
all your thoughts, words and deeds, and try
to make sure that you refrain from creating
negative energy with body, speech or mind.

Rinpoche also taught me how to create
extra merit - like skies of merit, he would
tell me; simply by turning prayer wheels
filled with mantras, by circumambulating
the stupa, by making tsa tsas (little Buddha
statues), by reciting mantras, by setting up
altars with Buddha statues known as the
rupakayas of Buddha deities. This, Rinpoche

said, manifests karmic merit which comes
from the blessing power of the Buddhas.

I soaked them all in, eager to please him,
but eager too to generate good energy. The
more Rinpoche revealed these teachings
to me, the more I came to realize that
they complemented all that I was doing
in feng shui. In fact, when I combined the
spiritual practices of creating merit with
my knowledge of feng shui, I came to
understand how enormously empowering the
spiritual practices were.

All images of Buddha deities, Rinpoche
explained to me, all stupas and prayer
wheels, all painted images and statues,
represent the Buddha's mind, known as
Dharmakaya.

These are holy objects, especially when
they are consecrated and filled with powerful
mantras. They bring incredible blessings
which come direct from the Buddhas.

Above: **In 2002 we produced a set of 21 Taras made of translucent resin which, when lit up, cast a glow so magical I made one set specially to offer to Lama Zopa and several more to present to friends who had strong affinity with the Goddess Tara.**

Far right: **Water bowls are offered daily to my 21 Tara altar in the East living room of my home. Making water bowl offerings create wonderful merit to attain Enlightenment.**

I have taken all Rinpoche's teachings to heart. Like a sponge, I soak up everything Rinpoche teaches me. The more I learn and implement and practice, the more Rinpoche teaches me… and each year, Rinpoche would come and visit me, stay with me… and I would also fly all over the world to receive teachings form him. Indeed I flew everywhere to see Rinpoche. Every spare moment I had, I would take off… and for over six or seven years, this was how I lived; earnestly chasing the Dharma. In the process, I received so many wonderful teachings, so many stunning practices, mantras, sadhanas… most of all I received so much blessings!

Turning My Home Into Pure Land

Over time without consciously realizing it, I was incorporating all Rinpoche was teaching me into the feng shui of my house. I discovered that I had a passion for Buddhist art. The colourful thangka paintings took my breath away.

I remember the first time I saw them, in Rinpoche's room at the FPMT center in Singapore, I felt an aching need to take them all home with me. Rinpoche must have read my thoughts because he said, "Here, choose one to take home with you." I could not choose because they were all so beautiful, but finally, I pointed tentatively to a stunning thangka of Four Armed Chenrezig…

That first gift from him started me on a joyous quest in search of the best thangkas I could find. So today, I have some very awesome thangkas, incredible works of art that are so fine, so painstakingly drawn with proportions so perfect that anyone looking at them cannot but be moved…

Many who have come to my home have fallen in love with my thangkas and I am glad of course. This creates powerfully positive energy and it also generates good karma. These thangkas are all consecrated and everyone can feel their blessing power. My mum who lives with me and who suffers from severe Alzheimer's seems very taken by them for she never fails to put her hands together in the prostration mudra each day

when she passes them on the way to the dining room. My grandson Jack is equally awed by my Buddha images. Every day he visits me and the first thing he does is goes before the Buddha images on my various altars to recite his mantras... He is five years old and he knows all the common popular mantras already.

Then of course there are my Buddha statues. I cannot resist them. I have big life-size statues from Thailand, Burma, Cambodia, Laos, Japan, India, Nepal, Tibet

and of course China. The large statues are displayed everywhere, in every room, and I have them sitting and standing with different hand mudras. These Buddha statues are all consecrated.

On my altars are statues that come mainly from **Katmandu** and **Tibet**, and these are made of brass or copper and then plated with gold. I have also gold leafed almost all the Buddhist statues which I revere as objects of refuge. These are filled with precious mantras and blessed by many high lamas,

have other high lamas. They feel comfortable here because I have not only designed my home to good feng shui, but have also filled it with thousands of holy objects so that every one of us living, eating, sleeping, playing, praying and working here are continually blessed, protected and guided by the Buddhas.

Somehow and without me planning to do so, over the past years, I have slowly and steadily filled my home with some **very precious holy objects**.

"These are wonderful ways to create merit," Rinpoche has repeatedly reminded me, "and each morning, all you do is look at your holy objects and place your hands together in the prostration mudra and then say a silent refuge prayer to the Buddhas." Rinpoche assured me that if I did my daily practices and meditations faithfully, the Buddhas would all reside in my home, in effect truly transforming it into a Pure Land! Perhaps that is why the flowers bloom so often and the trees grow so tall, and the leaves grow so waxy and so green. Maybe that is why the squirrels and the birds come, and the fish swim in such gay abandonment…

The energy of my home is incredibly empowering and I am sure that it is more than just the good feng shui. Sure, technically we enjoy excellent feng shui orientations, but the home also benefits from the blessing power of the holy objects.

Above: **Light and flower offerings, and the Tara prayer booklet we use when we conduct the Four Mandala Offerings to Cittamani Tara pujas on the 8th day of every lunar month. That is when the East hall of our home transforms into a pure land which creates exceptional chi energy for the home.**

Powerful Pujas Protect & Bring Prosperity

Living so intensely aware of Buddhist practices which Rinpoche has taught me, and having access to so much material supplied by the FPMT, I am now able to do regular pujas each month during the days of the new moon and the full moon, during days of the sun or moon eclipses and during special Buddha days. And on the 8th day of the new moon, I and my Buddhist pals prepare wonderful offerings and then sit and recite special prayers together.

Pujas are literally translated as "Offerings". So this is when we come together to make offerings to Buddha deities

and especially by **Lama Zopa Rinpoche**, who is my root guru now, my Vajra master and whom I love with great devotion. He is a living Buddha, a holy being who is so pure I just know that he has transformed my house into a veritable pure land, a place where everyone is happy, a place which attracts many visitors from all over the world, and also incredibly many very high lamas as well.

Since Rinpoche's first visit here twelve years ago, he has come many times, and so

Sure… technically we enjoy excellent feng shui orientations, but the home also benefits from the blessing power of the holy objects.

we pray to. Pujas are ritualistic, requiring knowledge of hand mudras and the usage of ritual objects such as the dorje and bell. All pujas require texts that have been translated from the sutras, and these comprise meditations, visualizations and the recitation of special mantras.

There are different pujas for different purposes and the more difficult pujas are done at the monasteries. But generally, pujas help you overcome obstacles, bring about healing for illnesses and protect against misfortunes, court cases and alleviate suffering brought by a variety of difficulties. Pujas are thus incredibly powerful as protection for the household.

There are also incense pujas that help you appease "local spirit landlords" and these are easy to perform as well as being extremely effective. Thus whenever there is disharmony in the home, doing incense puja can be effective. Usually, when something goes wrong in my household, I first check the feng shui - i.e. the monthly afflictions - after which I will also do an incense puja to appease surrounding spirits.

There are also pujas that invoke the help of wealth Buddhas and these are most helpful when it is done with the correct rituals. In the case of wealth deities, they usually require water offerings.

As for all other pujas, it is excellent to learn how to set up the altar offerings. Generally, we must include the five basic offerings and these are flower offerings, water bowl offerings, incense offerings, food offerings and light offerings...

Top: Jack enjoys it whenever Lamas come and visit.

Above: **With Khenrinpoche Lama Lhundrup** the Abbot of Kopan Monastery in Katmandu and my Buddhist friends Datin Pek Ling, Puan Sri Siew Yong, and MK Sen.

Facing page: I have received many precious teachings and initiations from the incomparable **Kyabje Choden Rinpoche** who came to stay in 2006 and is coming again in December 2009. I have also gone on two very meaningful Pilgrimages with Rinpoche and they were amazing spiritual experiences.

Flower offerings make you more beautiful; water bowl offerings reduce anger and emotional suffering; Incense Offerings clear obstacles: Food offerings bring wealth: Light offerings bring wisdom and clarity of thinking.

These offerings should be set up in a special altar before the start of pujas. We do pujas regularly as part of my personal Dharma Practice. These offerings of prayers do much to maintain the positive energy of the home, mainly because pujas are effective for keeping local spirits appeased and happy.

My Special Link With Charok Lama

Charok Lama is not only extremely bright and clever for his age, he also has great compassion, as well as a huge understanding of the modern world.

Above: **Charok Lama and I have wonderful conversations about just about everything and anything. Here I am in his room at Sera Je Monastery.**

In addition to Lama Zopa Rinpoche, I also have a very special connection with Charok Lama Rinpoche, a young reincarnate lama I met at Kopan Monastery in Katmandu also in 1997. He was five years old when I met him but the recognition here was as instant and immediate as it had been with Rinpoche. As soon as we met, he had come over to me, taken off my sunglasses and stared directly at me for several seconds before grabbing me in a bear hug... On my part, I loved him so much I wanted to bring him home with me. I wanted to adopt him, make him stay with me. It was absurd of course, because reincarnate lamas "belong" to the monasteries...

But I was lucky because Lama Zopa allowed me to sponsor his education and when he enrolled at Sera Jey Monastery in South India for the Geshe program, I decided to look after him. Each annual holiday, Rinpoche allowed Charok whom I nicknamed Charles to come and spend a couple of weeks with my family. As a result, Charles has become very close to me.

He is sixteen years old now and we have had wonderful conversations about almost everything these past ten years. I believe he will one day become a great lama because not only is he very bright and clever, he also has great compassion, as well as a huge understanding of the modern world.

But Charles is also extremely skillful in his interaction with others. I can see the way he has complete control over his mind and his attitude. For someone so young, he is incredibly well-disciplined.

In case I am making him sound like an icon of dull perfection, I must also add that Charles is also great fun, with a big sense of humour and great humility as well.

Vacationing with my Family

It must be that my family, Wan Jin, Chris, Jennifer and Jack all have strong karmic affinity with Charok Lama because come vacation time each year, they automatically think of him. This is because Charok has spent so many vacations with us these past ten years. We have followed his progress since getting to know him and when he enrolled at **Sera Je Monastery**, we worried about him, wondering if he could cope with the very tough and demanding regime of study there.

Although Charok Lama is a reincarnate lama recognized by **HH the Dalai Lama** and with heavy responsibilities on his shoulder, to us he is family, a young teenager who has blended in seamlessly with our family. Giving him a glimpse into the "real world" outside the monastery has been wonderful for him. There is no doubt in our minds that he is "special" not just because of his great intellect, but also because he is extremely gentle and so very humble.

There is an aura of purity around him that rubs off on us each time he comes to stay. We love him like our own and we look forward to the day when he takes his place amongst the great lamas of the coming decades. I know that he will teach my daughter and her family many things about Dharma.

Charok Lama's connection with Chris is also amazing to an extent that Chris once told him, " I want a son like you Charles!"

It is definitely not a coincidence then that in 2004, Chris got his wish, for that year, Jack was born and like Charok Lama, he was born in the year of the Monkey! Now as Jack grows up, I am amazed at the many mantras he has somehow picked up from me; and how each night he recites his mantras to sleep.

The great news is how well Charok gets along with Jack and each time he comes to visit, Jack follows him around, imitating everything he does. We are truly very blessed having this close link with such a special golden child.

Top: **Skiing in Vail with Charok Lama;** *Middle*: **In Hawaii he helped us mind Jack ;** *Bottom*: **At the Hilton Hawaiian Village in 2008.**

Khadrola Comes to Stay

And breathes some very special magic into our home! As soon as she arrived, Jack bonded instantly with her, following her around and never allowing her to get out of his sight, not even for a moment... And when we showed her to her guest room, Jack refused to allow anyone else to enter.

It was Lama Zopa Rinpoche who suggested that I invite her to my home, explaining to me just how special a lady she is. Amongst Buddhist circles, she is respected as a very highly realized woman, with highly developed skills in meditation. Rinpoche suggested that I could learn very much from her. Actually Rinpoche had suggested that she come some years ago but my good karma had not yet then ripened. It was only after my Prayer Wheel got built that all obsatcles to her coming were overcome and she made it here. For that I greatly rejoice.

She stayed with us for a week and during that time shared wonderful and precious insights with us. She taught us how to meditate deeply on the True Nature of the mind, leading us gently into a deeper understanding of Mindfulness and Emptiness.

It was awesome what Khadrola taught us. And when we did a Tara Puja together, the energy created was mind-blowing. We felt a lightness of being that for me personally, and for my friends was magical.

Khadrola also agreed to create and consecrate ten wealth vases of the Wealth Tara for my small group of fellow Buddhist practitioners. We refer to ourselves as a Mindful Alliance of Friends in Attainment, as we spend a great deal of quality time together travelling on pilgrimages, performing pujas and gilding the prayer wheel.

Having Khadrola in our midst made our small Alliance very meaningful indeed. And of course I forgot to tell you, she is a real life Dakini, and perhaps a Goddess ?

Top: Khadrola with me and my MAFIA friends - the "Mindful Alliance of Friends in Attainment." We benefited greatly from her visit and from her teachings on the Nature of the Mind.

Above: Making the WEALTH TARA wealth vases with Khadrola in my Meditation Room upstairs.

Facing page: Jack and Khadrola got on like a house on fire! When she came to visit, Jack followed her everywhere! He kept asking for her each day waking up early in the mornings to come and have breakfast with her. It was magical to watch them interact with one another. It was as if they had known each other for years. After Khadrola left, Jack insisted on learning all the mantras I knew and today he recites different mantras to sleep each night.

Boy Lama Phuntsok Rinpoche

Many years ago, when **Geshe Lama Konchog**, the revered **Mahasiddha** (highly realized being) from Kopan Monastery in Katmandu was in Singapore, I invited him to visit my home and to consecrate the stupa which Lama Zopa Rinpoche had sent to me. Geshe La agreed to come, but alas was not successful in getting his Visa to Malaysia. Definitely an obstacle had prevented him from visiting me.

When I spoke to him and expressed my regret, he replied, "I promise you I shall come and visit you one day..." Unfortunately that did not happen. Geshe Lama Konchog passed away some years after that, and when his body was offered to the fire, that was when all of us realized what a high practitioner he had been.

When Kopan monks searched through the ashes, there were so many beautiful pearl relics, hair relics and five colour relics, all of which indicated attainment of high status as a practitioner, someone very special... although in his lifetime, Geshe La had been humble and very low key.

Four years after he passed away, his reincarnation was found and in a colourful ceremony at Kopan, little Phuntsok Rinpoche was enthroned as the unmistaken reincarnation recognised by **HH the Dalai Lama** and by **Lama Zopa Rinpoche**. A year after his enthronement, he came to visit and stay with me here in Kuala Lumpur... that was when he whispered to me, "I'm keeping my promise to you." It just blew me away...

Top left: Phuntsok Rinpoche by the pool and mango tree in my garden.

Middle left: Jack at two and Phuntsok Rinpoche (4 years old) tentatively getting to know each other.

Bottom left: Phuntsok Rinpoche with his aunt at the front of my house, before the giant prayer wheel was built.

Facing page: Phuntsok Rinpoche at the number 11A house.

PART 8
SIGNING OFF ON A HIGH NOTE

We are coming to the end of the book and this is also the time for a fresh new beginning. Life goes through cycles of time, and endings merge seamlessly into new beginnings. Homes benefit from fresh energy each time a New Year comes round. This is generated from the creation of celebration chi by symbolic dragons, lions and phoenixes that prance around in a dance of auspicious rejuvenation.

This is the rationale behind the noise and the happy rituals that lie behind lunar New Year festivities which last for fifteen days, starting from the new moon and culminating on the night of the full moon, the fifteenth night. That is the time when homes should shine with new gloss and glow with bright lights. Yang energy gets created which hopefully lasts through the year... we also celebrate birthdays though never in a big way unless it is to mark an important milestone such as one's 60th which ends one complete Zodiac cycle.

COMING FULL CIRCLE

Dotting the Phoenix

Loud noise is excellent for generating yang chi which during the New Year period is always auspicious.

For many years, we used to only invite dancing lions to perform a variety of auspicious kung fu style dances as an offering to my Buddhas, and also to create fresh new energy for the home. The loud clashing of cymbals that accompanies the Dragon Dance is supposedly excellent for driving away all harmful vibrations and bad energy. Loud noise is excellent for generating yang chi which during the New Year period is always beneficial.

Everyone makes a special effort. In recent years, we have also taken to having the Dragon and Phoenix dance, as this is what generates harmony and smooth sailing. The Phoenix is yin and it brings opportunities, while the Dragon is yang bringing success. Together, they create the tai chi of heavenly

yin and yang, which transforms all mundane energy into empowering good fortune chi. Feng shui is always about engaging the energy from heaven because it is this that creates the trinity of tien ti ren, Heaven Earth and Mankind, which generates such excellent good fortune. In my home I observe all this and more. There is an abundance of heaven and earth luck and I make very sure that the mankind luck produced is always available.

Dressing Up for the New Year

New Year is the time when the home gets dressed up with plenty of red ribbons, lucky knots and auspicious rhyming couplets that are empowering Chinese affirmations.

Above: **Dotting the eyes of the Phoenix during Chinese New Year.**

Wealthy homes hang calligraphy of auspicious words that are specially written by esteemed masters and I always have them around the house during the New Year. I also hang plenty of red lanterns that somehow create a suitable ambience of celebration. They make the energy come alive with happiness.

The entrances of my home also get adorned with auspicious plants usually the Kuan Yin bamboo twisted to grow in an interwoven pattern that resembles the mystic knot. Sometimes they are also twisted into the powerful number of the year especially when the number is 8, a number embraced by all Chinese as the ultimate lucky number.

Another popular plant used during the new year to bring wealth into homes are miniature orange plants specially grown in nurseries and timed to bear fruit around new year time. Such plants are dripping with oranges to signify abundance. The Chinese word for oranges is kum which also sounds like the word for gold. Those in business believe very much in these orange plants, as do I. During the New Year, I place many orange plants all around my large home.

I also make plenty of offerings to the Buddhas - the same five basic offerings of flowers, incense, food and fruits; water and lights - that we offer during pujas. This is an auspicious time when invoking the Buddhas for blessings are especially beneficial. On the 8th day of New Year many families also pray to the God of Heaven. This is to ensure that business for the year continues to be blessed with success luck and that all obstacles get overcome with ease.

Pussy Willows bring New Growth

We are especially fond of the pussy willows as these signify the season of Spring. The ones I get are freshly cut from trees that grow in China and when soaked in water, our warm weather cause it to send wonderful green shoots that signify a successful start to the year. We usually look closely at how many of our pussy willow stalks send out shoots because the more they turn green to signify new growth, the more auspicious the indications are for the coming year.

As I am an enthusiastic gardener, I know that the way to make them send out shoots is to make a fresh cut on the stem just

Top: **Standing in front of my main entrance, which is flanked by two pots of magnificent Kuan Yin bamboo plants.**

Above: **It is always good to hang lanterns during the Chinese New Year.**

New Year is a time when the home should be dressed up with plenty of red ribbons, lanterns, lucky knots and ryhming couplets...

before soaking them in water. This enables the water to rise up the stalk causing it to begin its growth process. It should not be surprising then that my two urns of pussy willows which are decorated with lucky symbols always sends out a great many new shoots indicating that the coming year will be blessed with good fortune.

I have been decorating my home with pussy willows every New Year since my Hong Kong days, which is where I picked up many Taoist rituals of good fortune. For instance, I make sure that I wear a new red outfit on the first day, smile through the day and banish all negative thoughts from my mind. On my table will be laid out a variety of sweets and tasty cakes and biscuits. The table is filled to overflowing with yummy goodies and I have also made very sure that my refrigerator and my rice urn have been filled to the brim the previous night... entering the new year with the house filled to overflowing with wine and food is a must if you want the rest of the year to bring a state of prosperity and plenty.

I beat on my ritual drum each day for fifteen days, and I give traditional red packets filled with lucky money to my children and grandchildren; to everyone who works for me and also to those who come and celebrate New Year with me. We Chinese believe that during the new year is a very auspicious time to donate to charities and spread happiness to those who depend on one for sustenance by giving them red packets of money. They in turn should use the money to fill up their wealth vase.

Top: We hold our annual Feng Shui Extravaganzas in Singapore at the large convention hall in Suntec City mainly because the speaking direction is excellent for me based on my personal auspicious direction... so here I am with my husband and Peter Lung who usually flies in all the way from Las Vegas to support me. Peter is our partner in the United States and a long time feng shui friend...

Above: The picture here shows me with Surendran who is a very good friend from Bangalore. Surendran is a feng shui and Vaastu expert with a very successful consultancy business in South India. Next to him is GM Vincent Koh and G.Master Tan Koon Yong, two of Singapore's more prominent Feng shui experts, and betwen them is Eng; they organise the International Feng Shui Convention held annually in Singapore.

Facing page: At the end of the Extravaganza, it is 5pm, and my feet are exhausted.

Overleaf: Singapore Extravaganza 2009

My Feng Shui Extravaganzas

For the past ten years since my feng shui company was established I have been holding annual Feng Shui Extravaganzas in Kuala Lumpur, Singapore and also in the United States and either in Europe or Australia. The maximum I can do is four each January as they are timed to be held before the start of the lunar New Year. I use the Hsia calendar to time my talks because feng shui changes on the 4th of February the start of the Chinese Hsia calendar year. This is the day which corresponds to the day of Spring also known as the **lap chun day** of the year. When the actual lunar new day falls on a day after February 4th, this means the coming year lacks a lap chun, lacks a spring

and such years are generally regarded as unfortunate years when harvests will be poor and prosperity luck diminishes.

My Extravaganza presentations start at ten in the morning and continue on until five in the afternoon. It is a day when I saturate my audience with forecasts, predictions and a complete analysis of the coming year. This is when I am able to alert everyone to the feng shui afflictions of the coming year, and show them how to remedy these afflictions; how to place special enhancing symbols to overcome bad luck and attract good fortune. It is a fun day when I work at creating a carnival like atmosphere and show one and all how easy and fun using and applying feng shui should and can be.

The Extravaganza event is where I present specially researched and analyzed updates for each new year. I walk them through the new year's flying star chart and explain in depth the year's paht chee chart.

In addition to learning about the prospects for the coming year, the audience also gets exposed to how feng shui is analyzed and updated. Over the years my crowd has grown and each year we see more people. News of my event is advertised in our magazine **Feng Shui World** and on our website **www. wofs.com**. The crowd comes because word of mouth recommendation is especially powerful. This is an event I look forward to each year.

We have a great time!

That is when I connect directly with my readers, have a reunion with my students, some of whom go as far back as fifteen years. Many have been to my home and the earlier students are surprised at how the good energy of the home has just expanded exponentially. It is for them that I have written and produced this book. I know that many of you reading are wanting more, asking to see my upstairs and my bedrooms. But gee… some things in one's life really should stay private! It has been great fun doing this book with Jennifer & Chris and I wanted to end on a high note. If you want to find me, you can look for me on Facebook or you can subscribe to my weekly newsletter by registering via **www.wofs.com.**

Main picture: **Feng Shui Extravaganza in KL 2008, at the KL Convention Center.**

DEDICATIONS

To all you wonderful people who have come to study with me from around the world, my MPC, MCC, Paht Chee and Inner Feng Shui students who have become dear friends and business associates, I dedicate this book to you with love and prayers. I hope you have enjoyed this tour of my home and that for many of you, it brings back fond memories of good times held here.

May your practice of feng shui bring you joyousness and great fulfillment, in succesesfully helping others attract prosperity, satisfaction with their lives and good health. May you enjoy success and may all your wishes come true.

And with much love in my heart, I also dedicate this book to my fabulous family, my Mum, my husband Wan Jin, Jennifer, Chris, Jack and Josh; to my brother Phillip, nephew Han Jin, Audrey and Dom, niece Honey, Patrick, William and Ryan; and also to Connie, Nickque, Stanley, Janice, Andrew, Anthony, Kenji, Yew Sun, Gopal, Bernard and the many more at WOFS, too numerous to mention.

I love you all...
Thank you for believing in me and for being part of my Mandala.

Lillian Too